KEPT, SAFELY KEPT

Kept, Safely Kept

by

Adrian Ferguson

JOHN RITCHIE LTD
CHRISTIAN PUBLICATIONS

40 Beansburn, Kilmarnock, Scotland

ISBN-13: 978 1 907731 44 0

Copyright © 2011 by John Ritchie Ltd.
40 Beansburn, Kilmarnock, Scotland

www.ritchiechristianmedia.co.uk

Typeset by John Ritchie Ltd., Kilmarnock
Printed by Bell & Bain Ltd., Glasgow

Kept, Safely Kept

Kept, safely kept;
My fears away are swept;
In weakness to my God I cling,
Though foes be strong I calmly sing,
Kept, safely kept.

Kept by His power,
Whatever dangers lower,
The strength of God's almighty arm
Doth shield my soul from every harm,
Kept by His power.

Through simple faith,
Believing what He saith,
Unshaken on my God I lean,
And realise His power unseen,
But known to faith.

Kept all the way,
E'en to salvation's day,
His mighty love ne'er cold shall wax,
Nor shall His pow'rful grasp relax,
Through all the way.

William Blane (ca 1880)

Contents

Acknowledgements

The following pages tell a little of the life story of Audrey Ferguson – so far. We hope that this book will be of interest to a wide readership. If you find any pages overtly spiritual or overtly medical, please stick with them – they are part of the story. We hope that you will enjoy this book and feel that Audrey's story can be a help to you.

There are many people whom we acknowledge and to whom we are deeply grateful:

Dr Bert Cargill for his expertise in editing this book, and his wise counsel over many years.

Ian and Bitten Campbell for being our dear friends, through thick and thin. "A friend loves at all times." Proverbs 17:17

Jim McMaster for praying. God answered your prayers.

Robert and Jenny Thompson for making sense of all the confusing medical terms and opening their home to us.

Marian Rixham for opening her home to Adrian and Anna for five weeks.

The medical staff of Perth Royal Infirmary, especially consultant Dr Peter Brown who has been Audrey's consultant since diagnosis; Maureen Blair, respiratory nurse, for her dedicated care to Audrey, supported by the pulmonary rehab team at PRI.

The medical staff at Caledonian Road Medical Centre, Perth, particularly Dr Sharon Lee who has shown the utmost attention to Audrey's medical needs.

The medical staff of Freeman's Hospital, Newcastle, expertly led by Professor John Dark and Professor Paul Corris. This team includes surgeons, doctors, nurses, physiotherapists, nutritionists, social worker and transplant coordinators. Their dedication to Audrey and care beyond the call of duty makes us forever grateful.

The work colleagues of Adrian who covered his work load when he needed time off.

The LAM Action team for their support and help. The LAM community have stood together to help Audrey and others with this rare and debilitating disease.

Our many friends who prayed, wrote and gave of themselves to help us in our need.

Our families for standing by us at all times. When the going was at its toughest they were always there; especially John and Anna who for many years put their lives on hold to help Audrey.

Finally, to an unknown lady and her family, without whom this story would have ended in tears.

We welcome correspondence via the publisher.

Adrian & Audrey Ferguson
Methven, Perthshire.
August 2011

Foreword

Christian friendship is a sweet thing indeed, and occasionally some friendships transcend the normal level. Wise King Solomon spoke of this when he said, "There is a friend that sticketh closer than a brother" (Proverbs 18:24). This deeper friendship is graphically in evidence in the lives of David and Jonathan, of whom it was said, "the soul of Jonathan was knit with the soul of David, and Jonathan loved him as his own soul" (1Samuel 18:1). The 'knitting' of my close, deep, personal friendship with Adrian and Audrey Ferguson started at a summer youth camp at Pitlochry, Scotland in 1997. In previous months they had just suffered the heartache and heartbreak of the loss of a baby daughter, Anna, who was born prematurely, and it was shortly before that tragedy that Audrey was diagnosed with the rare, degenerative lung disease, LAM (*Lymphangioleiomyomatosis*). Two such heavy blows would have made many of us throw in the towel, but here they were at camp throwing themselves wholeheartedly into working with children and teenagers. Over the past 14 years of close fellowship, I have come to see, as have many others, that this highly commendable attitude and selfless enthusiasm for exposing young people to the gospel of God, is so typical of this remarkable couple.

As Audrey's condition worsened, and it seemed a transplant was inevitable, they were put in touch with the Freeman's Hospital in Newcastle upon Tyne, home ground for my wife and me. This put us into even closer contact. They would also spend a few days with us each Easter, keen to enjoy the ministry of the Word of God at the annual Tyneside Bible Conference. These times of fellowship further strengthened the close bond

11

of friendship between us. However, we could see on each visit a marked deterioration in Audrey's breathing. She was becoming increasingly dependent on oxygen. I would have to say to the credit of them both, that in spite of the overwhelming difficulties and anxieties that this disease brought, I never heard them complain once!

I recall the first occasion when she was rushed to Tyneside because a lung had become available for transplant. One can with difficulty imagine the multitude of raging emotions that must have throbbed in Audrey's mind as the ambulance raced her towards major invasive surgery. However, on arrival the transplant could not go ahead, and so Audrey crashed from the dizzy heights of expectation to the bitter depths of disappointment! Nor was this to be an isolated 'false alarm'. There were to be several! One week she was called to the Freeman Hospital *twice!* To say this was a 'roller coaster' experience would be a gross understatement! And so the waiting game went on.

The old adage, "Increasing years bring increasing memory loss", is true, as anyone over 50 will testify. However, there are some days from life's calendar that are written permanently into our memories. Advancing years can never erase certain unforgettable events. This was the Apostle Peter's experience. He was an old man when he wrote his second epistle, but as he reflected on the past, there was one event that was etched indelibly on his mind. It was as fresh and radiant to him as the day it had happened, and so he could write, "We were eyewitnesses of His majesty. For He received from God the Father honour and glory, when there came such a voice to Him from the excellent glory, This is My beloved Son, in whom I am well pleased. And this voice which came from heaven we heard, when we were with Him in the holy mount" (2 Peter 1:16-18). So vivid and real was the mount of transfiguration to Peter, that the memory of it, unblighted by several decades, went with him to the grave.

Tuesday, August 19th, 2008 is such a date in my experience. I received an unexpected text message from Adrian mid-morning informing me that Audrey was on her way to the operating theatre for the transplant! Late afternoon I received another text saying the operation was over and Audrey was doing well. Imagine my horror when, later that evening, I received a call from Adrian asking if we could come over to the hospital to support him, as Audrey's condition was causing the doctors some concern. My wife and I travelled over immediately and as we entered the small waiting room we could sense the tension and apprehension in the room. Other believers were there and earnest prayer was made to the Lord for Audrey's preservation and well-being.

Later that evening Professor Dark entered the charged waiting room to give Adrian the alarming news that all was not well with Audrey. His words are as fresh in my memory as when he spoke them! "Audrey is slipping away. If we leave her as she is she will die! I feel I must take her back down to theatre! However, we might well lose her during the operation!" It all seemed so surreal. Was this really happening? Hadn't medical knowledge and expertise made transplants a mere formality? Were we on the verge of losing our beloved Audrey? Further intense prayer was made at the Throne of Grace and once more the waiting game began! Each minute seemed like an hour. Imagine the draining experience for Adrian and the immediate family, as they tried to come to terms with the fact that, humanly speaking, Audrey's life was hanging in the balance.

Not wanting to steal Adrian's thunder, I must leave him to fill in the details of this absorbing story.

In the Gospel of John, chapter 11, we read, "a certain man was sick, named Lazarus, of Bethany". This man's sisters, Martha and Mary, deeply concerned for the wellbeing of their brother, sent to seek the Lord's help. Their message was simple but touching –"Lord, behold, he whom Thou lovest is sick." The Lord's reaction is noteworthy! He said, "This sickness is not unto death, but *for the glory of God*, that the Son of God might be glorified thereby." This statement might surprise some, but from it we learn that it is possible for illness and sickness to bring glory to God and His Son. I would, without hesitation, suggest that how Audrey and Adrian have coped with the trauma of this awful degenerative disease, both before and after surgery, has, in so many ways, brought glory to God. All those who know them will testify with one voice that this is so!

I heartily commend to you this book with its very moving 'human' story.

Ian Campbell
South Shields
July 2011

CHAPTER 1

"As tough as teak" - Some Family Background

A ferocious storm was brewing over the remote Scottish south west coast. It was January 1932 and it had already been a long and fearsome winter for the hardy residents of Portpatrick, a town sitting perched on the edge of the Irish Sea. If it was any closer it would be submerged in its freezing waters. From those waters in the 1930s many fishermen attempted to make a meagre living. Life was difficult for everyone in Scotland at this time - whole towns were devoid of young men, an entire generation wiped out in the horrors of the Great War. To compound matters, a devastating financial depression swept across the developed world, with life savings turning worthless overnight. Men literally begged for work. They would take any job simply to earn some money to feed their families.

The storm of 14th January 1932 came with a particularly vicious edge. Nothing could stand in its way as it built up over the Atlantic Ocean, swept over Ireland and rose again with renewed vigour across the Irish Sea to smash into Portpatrick. Windows were shaken in their frames, chimney pots were blown off roofs and the sea smashed against anything in its way. The gales beat against small wooden outhouses, literally blowing them apart, throwing debris high into the air. Rain came and compounded the misery. This was a night when no one was safe, even in the quaint whitewashed fishermen's cottages.

It was 2am when the phone rang. Sound asleep in the comfortable family home was John Campbell, coxswain of the Portpatrick lifeboat. The voice at the end of the phone said with panic, "Come now Jock, there's a ship in trouble!" Jock Campbell, as he was affectionately known, had been too young to fight in the war and was now one of the few young men the town could muster. Jock, though, was no poor substitute - he was a master of the seafarer's skill. He was soon given the great responsibility of being in charge of the lifeboat, often sailing through treacherous seas, ensuring the safety of his men and attempting to rescue those in peril on the sea.

The SS *Camlough* had set off early on the 13th of January for its regular voyage from Belfast to Birkenhead. It was a large but unglamorous vessel, with a dirty but valuable cargo of oil and coal, essential to fuel the shattered economy of the United Kingdom. Nothing could protect the *Camlough* from the horrors of that night. The wind had blown the vessel miles off course, its propeller helpless to shift its 540 tonnes of deadweight against the mountainous seas. It was rapidly approaching the treacherous coast of Luce Bay, a place where many lives had been lost on its unforgiving rocks. SS *Camlough* had entered the final moments of its voyage. Its crew of ten were facing certain death. The captain raised the alarm from his antiquated radio. A single flare was fired into the sky - "Call out the lifeboat" - it was the only hope for his petrified crew.

The flare was spotted and a rescue party headed by Jock was assembled. The *Camlough* was in trouble but it was nearly 40 miles away by sea. The sea might be too wild for the lifeboat, but Jock and his crew set sail. It was no night for nervous passengers. Jock battled through these fiercest of seas towards the stricken ship. Jock Campbell was a man who was described as being "as tough as teak", and nothing would dampen his enthusiasm for rescuing lives.

Jock was a man well acquainted with the "rescue business". Not only did he seek to rescue souls from the sea, but he had a passion in seeking to see souls rescued from their sins. As a young man Jock himself had turned from his life of sin, to trust in the sinless, perfect Son of God, the Lord Jesus. He had experienced the pleasures of sin, but left them behind to follow the Saviour of sinners. His lifeboat work was an extension of his love for the souls of men. CT Studd wrote words which could be said about Jock, "Some love to live within the sound of church or chapel bell; I'd love to run a rescue shop within a yard of hell." Jock was running a rescue shop within a yard of hell.

As the lifeboat *J&W* struggled through the waves, the crew of the *Camlough* grew increasingly desperate, fearing that they might not be rescued in time. After hours of sailing, the funnel of the Camlough was a welcomed sight in a wild sea. Jock tried a close approach to assess the situation. All the men were still safe in the ship but the ship was in grave danger. A line was thrown to the *Camlough*, "We'll tow you from danger," yelled the winch man. Quickly the *Camlough* crew tied the line, but within only a few minutes, the mighty sea snapped the line and the casualty headed faster than ever into certain destruction.

Jock quickly executed the highly dangerous manoeuvre of drawing alongside the *Camlough* and arranging a 'Breeches Buoy' between the two vessels. This ancient technique establishes a line between the ships so that men can cross from one ship to another. It requires the heart of a lion to cross the line, but few options remained for the panic struck crew. Jock stood watching as the first nine men were transported safely into the *J&W*. The last man though, was paralysed with fear. The weather was too fierce, the line was too fragile and lifeboat too small. He began his crossing but lost his grip seconds away from safety and plunged into the icy waters of the Irish Sea. Nine were safe in the lifeboat but one was facing certain death in the sea. Jock could not leave him to drown. He threw off his oilskins and dived into the sea. "Hold onto me!" he shouted as he grabbed the shaking mariner. A line was thrown from the lifeboat and both Jock and the tenth man were brought safe into the *J&W*. Jock had fearlessly risked his life so that another could live. He was reflecting on an even greater sacrifice, that of His Saviour, who had given His life as a sacrifice for our sin.

Back in the life boat it was no time for celebration. "Let's go boys," shouted Jock as he resumed his place in the wheelhouse for the journey back to Portpatrick. The daring adventure had lasted 12 hours, they had travelled 70 miles, and Jock could rest satisfied that ten men were spared from death that day.

The RNLI acknowledged Jock's bravery by awarding him one of their highest gallantry awards, the Institutions Bronze Medal for his skill and courage. The medal was presented by the Prince of Wales, the future King Edward VIII. As Jock stood briefly before the Prince he rejoiced that he knew personally the King of Kings.

After the adventures of January 1932, Jock continued to be coxswain of the lifeboat, retiring from it in 1945 with the great commendation of saving twenty seven lives in his tenure. In 1942, Jock and his wife Gertrude had a son, John, who was to be their only child.

In 1952, the Campbells moved a few miles across country to the county town of Wigtown, where Jock took ownership of a general ironmongery store, a traditional Scottish institution which stocked everything 'from a needle to an anchor'. No matter what was needed, Jock stocked it as a service for the community. The years of hard labour on the sea, however, had taken their effect on Jock and he had his first heart attack in 1959. The man as "tough as teak" was now a man with little strength and he could never work at his previous pace. The shop was sold and the Campbells moved off to Ayr to a quieter life again beside the sea.

Now that the business was sold, Jock could dedicate more time to his son John, and encourage him in his growing interest in the Lord Jesus. John had himself confessed his sins to the Lord and received God's free salvation. Not only was he following his father's footsteps, but he was following the Saviour's command – "Follow Me."

John was only 17 when they moved to Ayr, and instead of

following his contemporaries to the cinema and the dance hall he began to devote himself to the study of Scriptures. He struck up a good friendship with Jim Anderson of Annbank who encouraged him to become involved in the evangelism of Ayrshire. John would dash home from his job in the carpet factory to join a band of young men who preached in the Ayrshire villages. These young men travelled all over Ayrshire in an Austin A55 van they had purchased together. Armed with a fervent faith and trust in God they shared the "Greatest story ever told" with the local villagers. These were special days for John and his companions. Few of them had received any specialist Bible training, but they loved their Saviour and they wanted everyone to know about Him. Why should they wait until they were older? People needed saved now! This urgency and passion in soul winning became a characteristic of the young John Campbell. Jock and Gertrude sacrificed their comfort so that John could be supplied with the materials needed to encourage him in the work of God. It was a sacrifice they said was "well worth it".

* * * * * * * *

Meanwhile over in the village of Greengairs in Lanarkshire lived another remarkable couple, James and Lillias Penman. Jim and Lilly, as they were called, lived a very simple but happy life, in this predominantly coal mining community. Jim was a clay miner, spending hours underground in great discomfort digging out clay. The years after the First World War and into the Second World War, were marked by a growing number of people who were asking, "Where is God in our troubles?" To Jim and Lilly the answer would be to point them to the cross and remind them of the unfailing love of God.

In the 1940s, a travelling preacher, Mr Willie Wilding, came to preach the gospel in Greengairs. Conditions were very basic for the preacher, so much so that his helper Frank Haggerty slept in a store hut in one of the Christian's gardens! Hundreds of people were being faced every night with the claims of Jesus Christ. Soon like a fire blowing through the village, a great localised revival broke out with over sixty villagers coming in repentance to the Lord. So many members of the Orange Lodge were converted that the Orange Band was barely able to function. By today's population figures, nearly 5% of the villagers were saved at that time. Jim and Lilly were integral in this very special outreach into their own community.

When Jim and Lilly set up home, housing was difficult to obtain. The few homes available were reserved for former soldiers. They started their married life in a one-room house, which they used joyfully for God. Very soon they were blessed with three children and the one-room house was greatly overcrowded. But they still had room for the many young Christians they invited for regular choir practice, and the three children had great enjoyment listening to the beautiful songs ringing through their home. The Penmans had little of modern comforts, but their hearts were burning for God.

Despite their humble background, Jim and Lilly gave absolute commitment to their Lord and Saviour. The little Back Brae Gospel Hall was desperately in need of refurbishment, so Jim and his contemporaries rolled up their sleeves and repaired this centre of Christian service. These were people who worked all day in back-breaking labour in farms or coal mines, and yet had energy and zeal to serve their Master. For the Penmans, family life was inseparable from Christian life. Their little family would often sit listening to the stories from the Bible. Very soon, their oldest girl Anna learned to love the Lord Jesus. She, like John in distant Ayr, had answered the call of Christ, "Follow Me."

As the years rolled on, John Campbell and Anna Penman met at one of the Lanarkshire Bible Conferences. These conferences were convened primarily as an occasion for Bible teaching but they also became a meeting ground for many young Christians. Where better to meet a compatible partner for life than at a place where God is honoured and His Word is taught!

John and Anna soon fell in love and were married in 1964. After the wedding they set up a new home in Ayr and waited to hear what God would want of their lives. Doors were beginning to open for them in Christian service. The One who said "Follow Me" would soon be testing their obedience to His commands.

CHAPTER 2

Birth and New Birth

Life in Ayr for the newlyweds, John and Anna Campbell, was a very happy cycle of work, local evangelism and caring for the senior Campbell family. It soon became apparent to all who knew John that the Lord had given him an ability to explain the way of salvation in a powerful but uncomplicated manner. As his gift developed, people increasingly sought his help to reach out into their communities with the gospel. Lives were being changed in Ayrshire and God was demonstrating His love through John and Anna's special ministry.

For them, however, decision time had come. The Lord had given John a special work to do, but could they trust Him further and leave behind his comfortable job, and seek financial support only from God? They prayed earnestly that the Lord would show them the clear way forward. God answered their prayers in a way no one quite expected. Initially they wondered if they might be led to serve the Lord in the West African country of Ghana. A young man called Jim Assari had travelled from Ghana to Scotland to further his engineering studies. John befriended Jim at his work. Soon he was delighted to learn that Jim had trusted Christ for salvation. Was this guidance from God that Ghana was for them? Around the same time, Jim Anderson compiled a small magazine to report on evangelism in Scotland. One comment was, "lots of activity in ...Fife, Renfrewshire, Aberdeenshire but what about Perthshire? Who will take up the challenge?" As John and Anna read these words, their challenge burned into their minds. The more they tried to discount it, the less they were able to forget it.

Over 100 miles north east of Ayr, a tiny congregation of Christians gathered in a sparse rented room above a shop in the town of Perth. This group had been in existence for nearly 100 years, but they were still very small numerically. In their weakness they began to pray that God would revive His work in Perthshire. Back in Ayr, God started to reveal to John and Anna that He was calling them to "Follow Me" to Perthshire, leaving behind family, jobs and comfort to serve Him in this rural environment. Making contact with the Christians in Perth they found them very open and receptive. When God called, they responded with the lovely scripture response, "Here am I send me."

John and Anna Campbell settled in Perth in 1967, moving into their new home in Priory Place along with their first child Lorna. She was quickly followed by Ruth, Hazel, Moira, and finally in 1972, Audrey - five girls all born in a seven year period. Life was seldom quiet in the Campbell household.

Priory Place became a centre of Christian witness and love. Barely a day went by without some sort of guest being welcomed. Many stayed in the small terraced home, with some guests staying for months on end. For the girls, they just had to crush together, five in one room, to allow their visitors to have a guest room. They used to whisper to each other at night, "When are they going?" "I don't even think Mum and Dad know," was the reply. Anna bore the bulk of the homemaking, soup was constantly on the hob, pancakes were freshly made, and the Sunday stew often stretched further than was imaginable. Rice pudding, a favourite with the girls, could be made to stretch a long distance as well. Conditions were basic but love abounded. Christmas time at the Campbells was an astonishing sight, every space on the walls decorated by the many hundreds of Christmas cards coming from friends all over the country. It had been only a few years since they had left Ayrshire, now God had expanded His blessing upon them and helped them settle into a new community.

One of the first priorities for John was to start reaching into the many small villages of Perthshire. Robert Gibson, a talented joiner friend from Ayrshire, set about the task of building a mobile Gospel Hall. This building was innovative as it could be dismantled, moved and erected in less than a day. The hall was so well built it was even suitable for use all year round, even in harsh Scottish winters. Thus John, accompanied by many willing volunteers, commenced pioneer evangelism to the long neglected Perthshire communities. For John, mornings were spent in correspondence and Bible study, afternoons were devoted to visiting village people, and evenings were spent preaching in these communities. Sometimes the meetings were held in such remote locations that the only guaranteed audience was John and his fellow preacher. These were tough days but the Lord began to bring a number of these contacts to faith in Christ. Slowly rural Perthshire was having little groups of Christians who could trace the commencement of their spiritual journey to a contact with the Portable Gospel Hall.

The evangelism of John and Anna was tireless and definitely exhausting. The Portable Hall moved location every 8-10 weeks. It was taken down section by section, loaded onto a lorry and built up again section by section. John was constantly looking for team members to set up the hall. "Get the foundations right," was his watchword, as the advance party set off to level the site and prepare the way. Long before recycling became the vogue, the Campbells had mastered it, not a screw was wasted and even the waterproof tape was reused at every move. In the hundreds of moves of the Portable Hall seldom was a person ever injured, but all slept well the night after a big move!

Throughout the late 1960s John had worked with a number of people, but in the 1970s Jack Hay of Prestwick relocated to Comrie and formed an enduring partnership with John. As well as preaching to children and adults, Jack would have the responsibility of playing the organ every night in the services. The small wooden organ, definitely a remnant from a previous era, was powered by bellows which Jack pedalled with his feet while playing the notes with his fingers. There was no need to visit a fitness centre - Jack's enthusiasm at the organ kept him fit!

The most popular services were invariably the Children's Bible Hour. John and Jack reached many families through initial contact with their children. The children would gather at the door, waiting for the joyful moment when it would be opened and they could take their places, boys on the right, girls on the left. In line with his thrift, John devised an ingenious points system to reward the children. Each was given an attendance card which would get a hole punched into it if they scored a point. Sometimes, though, the children were so keen and had earned so many points that the card almost disintegrated and the Campbell girls had the onerous task of trying to work out how many points would be in that missing square centimetre! The large attendance brought a very expensive monthly bill for prize books and sweets, but God again supplied every need without having to ask anyone else for resources to be provided. Some of the children's teenage brothers and sisters came to the teenage meeting, and after the Bible talk they would sit and enjoy friendly chat, asking challenging questions along with delicious juice and biscuits. Some of the wildest teenagers became marvellous examples of what God can do in people's lives.

Occasionally the weather turned sour during the Portable Hall meetings. One evening with the congregation inside the hall, a fearsome wind blew up and the hall started to creak in the wind. Suddenly one of the large metal-clad roof panels started to move. These panels were so heavy that it normally took four men to lift them. With the preaching in full flow, John had no desire to abandon the service. The answer quickly came from one of the young converts, a lad called Dave Martin. As a young lad, Dave had come to the Portable Hall to mock the Christians, but wherever his family seemed to move to, so also did the little wooden hall. Dave eventually received the Lord Jesus as his Saviour and became a fervent follower of Jesus Christ. That night Dave slipped out of the back door of the hall into the dark and wild night. He scaled the drain pipe, crawled over the roof, and found the loose roof panel. He lay over it, facing the mighty gale. He held on to it until the preaching was over! Dave concluded that his risk and sacrifice were worth it for his Lord.

The impact that the preaching in the Portable Hall had in those pioneer days, is still evidenced by the many individuals who still phone, write, or meet John and Jack. These friends speak passionately about how a certain message in the Portable Hall spoke to their hearts and changed their lives. The well worn cliché could apply, "Eternity alone will reveal the impact that this work had in the hearts of people."

One such family which benefited immensely from the Portable Hall evangelism was the Ferguson family. In the early 1970s George and Jean Ferguson had relocated from the city of Dundee to Perth as George had taken up a new job in a textile factory there. The factory and their home were within a few hundred metres of where John and Jack had set up the Portable Hall for another mission. One of the members of the Gospel Hall visited the Ferguson family and to their surprise, here were also four enthusiastic children who were interested in what was going on near their home. "Come along and bring your children," was the friendly invitation. It was a great joy to the preachers when George and Jean and the three oldest boys, Peter, Christopher and Jeffrey all started to attend the little hall. Their youngest child, Adrian, was only three - too young to attend the children's services. At least he could learn the songs when his brothers returned home each evening. Imagine the joy when the "wee one" heard that he could go on the prizegiving night and sing alongside his brothers like the rest of the "big ones"!

The Campbells diligently kept contact with the Fergusons for a long time after the Portable Hall had moved to a new area. One evening the Fergusons were invited to the Campbells for the first time. "Come and meet the girls," was the invitation from John. John was so proud of what he called his "six girls". This first visit to the Campbells home would be the first time that Adrian would set eyes on Audrey. Being brought up in a house of boys, he didn't know too much about how to play alongside girls, or play with dolls. So within seconds of introducing himself to the girls they had run away upstairs not to be seen for the rest of the evening. Adult company was going to have to do for Adrian that night! Within a short time the Ferguson family had started to become regular attendees at Perth Gospel Hall, and the boys became integrated with the other families of young people who were such a part of the growing Christian community in Perth at that time.

Whenever there was a free day the Campbell family loved to be occupied in some sporting activity. The youngest girl, Audrey, like all her sisters, also developed some sporting ability. She loved tennis and table tennis, and represented the school in both the volleyball and netball team. When she went to secondary school she started to play hockey and compete in athletics. Life was exhausting just watching the Campbell family rush from meetings, to school, to sports activities, to friends' houses, to having visitors.

Anna's young sister, Joyce was a favourite visitor. She would dash straight up from her work in Airdrie and burst into the Campbells' home always full of tricks and jokes. The girls would eagerly await her next visit and all the joy she would bring. They would sit and whisper to each other about the man that Joyce would soon marry, and laugh that their Aunt Joyce had finally met someone. The bad news was she would be moving far away. "Please come and stay at Christmas," the girls would plead.

To add further to the hectic preaching schedule, some of the Perth friends decided to form a Christian Camp for the young people who attended the Portable Hall. This camp was traditionally held in Aberdeen and always happened immediately prior to the Campbells' annual holiday. So after a full week preaching, teaching, counselling, cooking and organising games, John and Anna packed the girls in the car and drove all night from Aberdeen to Portsmouth. Often their destination was Jersey, Newquay, the Isle of Wight, or Portsmouth itself. This was family time and was essential in renewing their strength for the busy months ahead.

One Sunday night in January 1980, Audrey's family had all been to the Gospel meeting in Perth. Most of the family had come home to get ready for school the next day, but her sister, Moira, decided she was going on to the Portable Hall meeting afterwards with her Dad. When they came home, Moira was clearly very distressed and she went to the front lounge for a discussion. When they came through to the sitting room, Moira told her Mum and sisters that she had just trusted the Lord for salvation. Everyone was delighted including Audrey. But when Audrey tried to go to bed that night she could not sleep because all she could think of was that most of her family were now saved and if the Lord Jesus was to come again she would be left behind. Audrey's sisters took her downstairs to talk with her parents as she was very upset. After confirming that this was a genuine desire for salvation, both her Mum and Dad were delighted to lead her to the Lord. As a girl of eight years old she gave her life over to Christ for Him to become Lord of her life. A burden was lifted from Audrey's heart. She slept soundly that night knowing all was well for eternity.

Audrey's simple trust in God would be put to the test daily in the many trials she was just about to face.

CHAPTER 3

Growing in Faith

For Audrey, this new disciple of Jesus Christ, there seemed little point in being half hearted about her Saviour. Her friend Susan was the first to hear her news, "Susan, I've become a Christian, I've been saved." Susan smiled, she was so pleased for Audrey but she was also puzzled - wasn't Audrey already brought up as a Christian? Audrey was soon to demonstrate that real living faith is not a nominal or cultural thing, but an active walk with the living God.

One day, Audrey gathered her sisters and the Hay girls together to the front room of Priory Place. "We're going to play at Bible conferences today," she said. They scoured the house for the latest shopping catalogues and diligently cut out a whole congregation of faces from these glossy publications. They then sat these faces in rows on the carpet, and in their young minds they were ready to start the conference. But they needed a preacher! The choice was unanimous, "It has to be Audrey," they said. The eight year old preacher stood up to address her audience. She looked over the sea of faces, and started to imitate the sermons of her father; "Are you saved?" she powerfully said, and hammered her fist against the lectern for effect. The audience of paper faces were expressionless - no response, so Audrey repeated some verses she had been memorising, "You must be born again" and "For God so loved the world ..." "It was a good sermon," the girls concluded, and now they would need to have communion just like their parents did every week. Quickly some blackcurrant juice and bread were found and the girls celebrated 'communion' together, just like what their parents loved to do.

As Audrey was growing up, Perth Gospel Hall ran a large and successful Sunday School. The Campbell girls, alongside the two Hay girls, occupied their own row at the back of the upstairs room. They were turned out beautifully each week for the Sunday School, with their long flowing hair, matching berets and pristine white ankle socks. If a question was asked, their hands would shoot up. The years of listening to their mother's stories and their father's preaching had taught them much from the Bible. However, they had a peculiar shy streak, but if no one else knew the answer they were certain to know. Their shyness, though, was cast away when their favourite quiz was conducted – Bible Sword Drill.

The main proponent of Bible Sword Drill was another new face to Perth, Willie Revie. Just a few months after John and Anna had moved to Perth, Willie and Annie Revie also moved to Perth from Ayrshire. Willie and Annie immediately got involved in this new pioneer work and soon the Sunday School would be operated primarily by Willie and a team of helpers. He was a man with a great love for the children, and his insatiable smile melted the hardest of hearts. Out in his minibus he started picking up children from the poorest of backgrounds. He would visit their homes, walking past the drunk on the stair well, past the glue sniffer and the bags of litter and filth to bring the message of salvation to these children. The children were packed into the minibus years before any laws on safety belts were enforced. They would head back to the Gospel Hall with perhaps thirty or more children crammed into that bus. The Lord mercifully kept them from injury or accident.

Back in the Hall, Willie would stand up and tell some anecdote related to his work with animals, perhaps about a lost sheep, or a good shepherd. The children sat spellbound as the stories were related to the messages of the Bible. Then it was quiz time, and the Campbell girls were on full alert hoping it would be Sword Drill. Willie would say, "Today's quiz is Sword Drill!" The girls wanted to jump for joy, but years of sitting still in conferences had taught them to contain their excitement. The instruction was given to 'draw their swords', and then repeat the Bible verse which they were to search for. After a pregnant pause Willie shouted – "Charge!" The children frantically searched their Bible index for the obscure verse that had been announced, but before anyone could find it, one of the Campbell girls was on her feet. Soon it would be Audrey, racing her sisters to be first with the answer.

In those early years, the Christians were very kind to Audrey, including her in all the activities of the Perth Gospel Hall. To ensure that all these young Christians could meet other young Christians at Bible conferences, a few of the leaders decided to purchase minibuses instead of cars. One of the elders, David Wilson, got an old German, left-hand drive army van, and used this as a minibus. The old van seemed to be an unusual cross between an ice-cream van and an ambulance, but at least there was plenty space to cram people in. One night as the young people were returning from their Bible study, David spotted a single wheel racing ahead of his van, and it looked remarkably like one of his van wheels! The wheel nuts had worked themselves free and the wheel had detached and continued forward at great momentum. Stopping was going to be a challenge. "Everyone lean left," he shouted, as the van slowly came to a stop resting on its other three wheels. Now they had to find the fourth wheel, minus bolts, and somehow fix it back on to the van. "Take one bolt off each wheel," David said, and a willing team of budding young motor mechanics reassembled the minibus. Soon they were back on their journey with another exciting story to talk about at Bible Class.

Sitting near the front of the Gospel Hall each week was Adrian, the youngest of the Ferguson family. He had hardly even found the index of the Bible, and never had much hope of beating the Campbells in Sword Drill, but at least it could be an aspiration. Week by week he started to memorise the Bible book order. His parents even gave him a Bible with handy thumb tabs to find the passages quickly. He was going to at least try and beat them at Sword Drill. This healthy competition made Adrian start noticing this family and admire their dedication to the work of God. But he could hardly even imagine that one day 'wee Audrey' would be his devoted wife.

When Audrey started school, the teachers enquired, "Are there any more girls?" Her four older sisters were already in the same school, and had been making a big impact. Lorna had excelled in art, Ruth was vivacious, Hazel was intellectual, Moira was a sports champion and Audrey seemed to have a combination of her sisters' attributes. She sat quietly, barely noticed by the teachers, but soon it would be sports time and Audrey was to learn to punch far above her weight. When it was time for the annual trials to pick the netball team, whilst younger than the majority of the team, she tried her best to get chosen. She dashed around the court, jumping high to catch the ball, spinning quickly to outwit her marker, and passing the ball to the attacker to score a point as the ball flew into the net. Audrey was an instant pick. This little powerhouse was exactly the kind of player the school team needed. When the summer months came, athletics took place in the field next to the school. The school was located in a large residential area of Perth, but the neighbouring building was the cattle and sheep market. The audience at the school sports was often supplemented by a runaway sheep or even on occasions a bull. Everyone would then retreat indoors. Back on the athletics track, Audrey sprinted around, digging deep into her resources and despite her petite frame she gave her utmost against far larger challengers. She did not always win, but she certainly gave it her best shot. On a Saturday, John would often book a badminton court at the local Sports Centre and the girls would be challenged to beat their father. Moira came closest, with her defensive style. "I'll wait for Dad to make a mistake," she said, and just when it happened, Moira pounced in for the winning point. Audrey admired her sister, "Hopefully I'll be able to beat my Dad soon." But Audrey was soon to learn that perhaps that would be a bigger challenge than she could have imagined.

Just as Audrey was entering her teenage years, one of her great examples of practical Christian living was to be taken away from her. Annie Revie was a lady who had devoted her life to the service of God, her family and to others. Each week Willie and Annie would open their home to the Christians both in Perth and from far further afield. They were extremely busy with their own five children and often they also looked after a nephew while his parents served as missionaries in Ethiopia. Annie was a lady whom all the Campbell girls looked up to as a role model. But then the shocking news came that Annie had terminal cancer. She grew weaker every day but still delighted to hear about others. Just a few days before her death, Peter Ferguson took his youngest brother Adrian to visit Annie. Adrian had never seen the ravages of cancer before. As he entered the room, he had never seen such weakness, and yet in the midst of it all here was a woman at total peace – her sins were forgiven and she was looking forward to being at home with her Lord. She was at the end of her life but was showing a deep interest in this young boy standing before her. Annie died just a few days later, and her youngest son Philip greeted Adrian almost joyfully with the news, "Mum went home to be with the Lord today." The family had learned to allow God to take home one whom He loved and who loved Him. For young Audrey, Annie's death raised great questions: "Why did God take Annie?" and "Who will be a role model for me now?" But very soon the Lord would send others to encourage her in her growing faith.

The Sutherland family became hugely influential to Audrey. Bill and Margaret lived Christ. They came from a Presbyterian background, which was quite different to many of the other members of the Gospel Hall. They lived a devoted Christian life and set an example that inspired all the younger Christians to be more devoted to the Lord Jesus. Just as Audrey started the Bible Class, Bill began to take one of the Bible discussion groups. Audrey would sit and listen to his explanation of the Bible, and then would watch with amazement as Bill tried to get the young people active in praying. He would end his lesson, and then turn round to one of the young men and say, "You close in prayer." Before the lad had time to refuse, Bill would have his head bowed as he waited for the prayer to commence. For many young men in the Gospel Hall that was their first experience of public praying. Dave Martin, the hero of the portable hall roof, cornered Bill one day. "Don't ask me to pray, I won't do it!" That very Sunday, Bill with his unique approach, turned and said, "Dave, you pray!" The reluctant Dave began praying and has since been a help himself to many young Christians in their prayer life.

It wasn't just praying that the Sutherlands engaged in, they had a real desire to tell their neighbours of God's love. David their second son, decided to organise a little tract group consisting of himself, Audrey and Adrian. "We'll visit every home in a large estate in Perth," David said with great zeal. Every week the little group went out to speak to people about the Lord Jesus and occasionally they would find someone who was keen to learn more about what they had to say. Bill and Margaret patiently waited at home, anticipating the latest updates on those who had been spoken to so that they could pray for them. Once the praying ended, the table was spread with lovely food and Audrey just sat and marvelled as the three big strapping Sutherland boys demolished a tableful of food. The Sutherlands still delight to remember these happy days, and when Audrey visits their home now Margaret spreads the table with the same type of delicious food that was enjoyed all these years ago.

A young couple who showed great kindness to Audrey and Adrian in their formative years were Graeme and Lillian Lamont. They were newly weds who had recently moved to the area, but they were delighted to open their home after every meeting to the young people in Perth. This gave a great opportunity to discuss the Scriptures and to help formulate their own convictions on spiritual matters. The young people felt loved, safe and encouraged by the Lamonts' sacrifice and dedication to them.

St Andrews was another place where Audrey learned something of involvement in Christian evangelism. In St Andrews Gospel Hall there was a very small congregation, probably with never more than eight members. Most of that time there was only one male, Mr Ian Ross, who conducted nearly all the services himself. Ian Ross was a unique character. He had had a wild upbringing, and left home fairly young to join the army. He married a German girl, Christa, which considering the bitterness of the 2nd World War was a brave thing to do. Not long after their wedding, Ian was posted to the war zone of Aden (now Yemen). In the pressures of a war zone, Ian started to contemplate ending their short marriage but God had other plans! Back in Scotland God had started working in the life of Christa. She had been invited to the Billy Graham All Scotland Crusade in 1955, and on the steps of the Kelvin Hall, Christa repented of her sins and became a follower of Jesus Christ. Her life was immediately changed. The Lord was now in control and she sought to remedy their marriage difficulties. She sat down and penned a letter to Ian. After several days the letter arrived in Aden and Ian began to read. She commenced with a verse of scripture, "There hath no temptation taken you but such as is common to man: but God is faithful, who will not suffer you to be tempted above that ye are able; but will with the temptation also make a way to escape, that ye may be able to bear it."

She began the letter, "My Dear Ian", but before he had read another word, a deep conviction of his own sin swept over him, and he cried out to the Lord for salvation. His words were rather unconventional but the Lord answered it marvellously: "Lord, if there is a way of escape – I'll take it now." Ian and Christa were now united in the Lord. Soon they would be back together in Scotland serving the Lord in the ancient city of St Andrews. One of the events they organised was the annual July outreach week, with volunteers from all over the UK coming to help in their mission team. Audrey signed up to help in the 1990 team, timed to occur during the world famous Open Golf championship. Ian and Christa courageously led during the mission week. They had gained so much experience and delighted to share it with young people like Audrey.

Audrey, though, had never experienced anything like it before – house after house of people completely disinterested in her Saviour. They had nice houses, good jobs, many were academics and thought they had no need of the Saviour. It was very hard ground for the Good Seed to find root, but almost every year some did find root and someone trusted in the Saviour. One year a curious tourist just passing the hall accepted the invitation to listen to the Gospel. The message was exactly what he had been seeking for and before he had even left the hall he had placed his faith in the Lord Jesus. He returned to his holiday caravan to tell his wife that he had been saved and to show her the Bible he had received from the enthusiastic young people at St Andrews. His wife seemed to accept her husband's conversion, but what about that Bible? "Take it straight back, it is not a real Bible - it doesn't say Holy Bible on the front." So the new convert returned, rejoicing in his Saviour but desperately in need of a Holy Bible.

In 1993 they received an invitation to come and attend a special young people's outreach weekend in North Shields near Newcastle. Audrey was keen to go, so Adrian borrowed his mother's Austin Metro. Adrian, Audrey and two friends headed south full of excitement. Just a few miles north of the final destination the Police put on their blue flashing light and pulled over the car of youths. The primary concern of the Police was not the speed they were travelling, but they wondered what this group of young people were doing in a car – surely they are up to something suspicious. "Where are you off to?" the Police Officer demanded. The reply came, "We're off to a Bible study." Since it wasn't a crime to study the scriptures the Police Officer quickly ran out of excuses and sent them on their way. Further surprises were waiting for them at North Shields. Just as they drew into the street and headed in to the Bible study, a friendly voice shouted, "Never leave anything visible in the car!" The young Scots began to wonder what kind of place they had come to!

After another enjoyable evening, everyone settled down to try and get some sleep. Just as the boys were dropping off to sleep on the wooden floor, one of the visitors began to sing hymns in a most beautiful voice. The leader was enthralled that here were young people who wanted fun but were also happy to praise the Lord.

When the morning came, the boys decided to check on the cars. "Oh no! – where had the Metro gone?" It had vanished. With horror they noticed at least two other cars had been broken into and things stolen. Audrey, Adrian and their friends were now stuck in North Shields minus the car – it wasn't even Adrian's property to lose! The usual phone calls to the Police station were made, but no car was found. Jim McMaster, the organiser, decided to take the Perth friends on a highlights tour of North Shields looking for the car. As they passed through the streets, it was soon obvious how different from rural Perthshire was life in the North East of England. One man was stealing paving slabs off the street, probably to build a nice patio at home, while many cars had permanent wheel clamps to stop them being stolen! This rude awakening was the beginning of a life saving connection with the Newcastle area for Audrey.

The main event of the day, though, was the Open Air preaching down at the Quayside. The weekend coincided with the Tall Ships Race, which was the biggest ever Tall Ships race in the UK. There were approximately one million people lining the Quayside watching the ships leave for their race at sea. Adrian watched in trepidation as Jim got out the Public Address system and started looking for volunteers to preach the good news of the Saviour. What a relief when someone else was chosen. Then again, another willing volunteer was found. As Adrian steadied his nerves he started to notice that the further they walked, the bigger the crowd seemed to become, and his excuses not to preach were starting to run out. Jim looked, "Adrian would you preach a message?" Adrian looked up, and in front of him was a crowd which may have exceeded 100,000 people. Adrian shook with fear but counted it a great privilege to be able to speak even falteringly of his Saviour before such a vast crowd. Audrey remembered the lessons she had learned in her formative years and she stood silently praying that God would bless the message that Adrian gave.

As everyone started to get ready for the evening meeting, the good news came that Mrs Ferguson's car had been found just a few streets away. As Adrian was a student, he had left only enough petrol in the car for a few more miles, and the joy rider had decided he wouldn't get much of an escape in a little Metro without any petrol! The car was returned, then Audrey and her friends headed home happy after another experience serving the Lord.

These happy days were great training for the momentous days that lay ahead.

CHAPTER 4

Falling in Love

Failing in love wasn't at the top of Audrey's priority list. She had a busy and fulfilling life and there would be plenty of time to meet her perfect man later. Home life for Audrey, though, was starting to get quieter. Her sisters all started to fall in love and the family home which had been such a centre of activity was becoming more tranquil. Then suddenly the tranquilly was shattered and the house was brought alive again, when Ruth's daughter Sarah was born, John and Anna's first grandchild. Audrey soon became Sarah's favourite. "Ruth, I'll change her nappy", "Ruth, I'll feed her," said Audrey, desperate to fuss over Sarah.

While Audrey was spending so much time with her little baby niece, boys were starting to admire Audrey. She was young and beautiful with lovely natural curly hair and a constant smile. She was quiet but not shy and loved to chat as long as someone else started the conversation. On the 14th of February, St Valentine's Day, the postman delivered the mail to the Campbell's home and Anna noted, "Three cards for Audrey!", "She's very popular." Audrey dashed down the stairs to get a pleasant surprise, three beautiful cards all from secret admirers. Her sisters started to have great fun speculating who were Audrey's secret admirers, but Audrey was patient - she wanted God to give her a suitable partner for life.

One of these youthful admirers was Adrian Ferguson, a lad Audrey had known for many years and who had really started to take a special interest in her. With the long summer holidays, Adrian would cycle across Perth and past the Campbell's garden, hoping for a glimpse of Audrey. She would invariably be in the garden practising tennis, hoping for a glimpse of Adrian. He would slow his bike and wave up to Audrey who would leave her tennis racquet and come for a chat before he would dash off again, with hope in his heart that perhaps he would be able to see her again soon. Occasionally Anna would look out to see who Audrey was talking to. The young ones were caught, and Anna would rush down. Adrian wondered if he would be chased away, but Anna just turned and said, "Come in for some tea and biscuits." Very soon Anna had found a job for Adrian - weeds were being pulled out of the large garden, or the grass was being cut. "Would you like a help another day?" offered Adrian, and Anna welcomed his offer. For Anna, he would be a helpful but particularly unskilled gardener; for Adrian it would be an opportunity to get to know Audrey a little better.

In the summer of 1988, Jonathan Sutherland invited Adrian to the Garden Festival in Glasgow. This was a spectacular event for Scotland, which had transformed a derelict dockland site into a major tourist attraction. The site boasted lush gardens, futuristic houses, roller coasters and beautiful views of the River Clyde. The Festival was an instant success with over 4 million people coming to visit it during the few months in which it was open. Jonathan, though, wasn't concerned about the flowers, he had match-making in mind, and unknown to Adrian, he had also invited Audrey. Jonathan turned into Audrey's street and Adrian's heart leaped – "Wow! a day out with Audrey," he said silently. They chatted all day, getting to know each other and slowly being drawn closer together.

Young love for Audrey and Adrian wasn't a thoughtless friendship, both had been praying that God would give them a partner for life, one who would be a real help in their walk for God. Their relationship took a long time to germinate, "Why hurry though we're still young," they thought, but their friends started to get curious, "Are they an item?" For the young friends, the Lord had continued to direct them into a closer friendship, and John and Anna seemed delighted to have an extra one in their family again.

On January 1st 1989, John and Anna arranged to take their minibus to Motherwell for a Bible conference. The seat beside Audrey was vacant, so Adrian seized the opportunity to sit with his now very close friend. After the conference, their interest in each other had moved a little deeper, and Adrian reached out his hand and took Audrey's. "What would her reaction be?" wondered Adrian, but Audrey responded by holding onto him. The journey seemed so short for them, "That cannot be Perth already?" they thought, as John pulled up his van outside Adrian's house. He ran into the house, floating on air, so delighted that Audrey was becoming more than just a friend. He started to wonder, "When can I see Audrey again? Perhaps she would like a long walk in the countryside?" He plucked up the courage and asked if she would come for a walk around the beauty spot of Kinnoull Hill. She was delighted to have a walk, especially after a few days sitting indoors. The two friends set off, safe that no one else knew about their blossoming relationship. The secret, though, was quickly revealed as two of the Gospel Hall members and their extended family spotted them, "Oh what's this they enquired?" The young couple blushed, but were proud of their new special friendship. The news started to spread as their friends began to talk, "Did you hear, that AA no longer stands for the Automobile Association!" Then they laughed, "It stands for Adrian and Audrey!" Soon wherever Audrey was Adrian came as well.

During these early days of their growing relationship, the Christians showed remarkable kindness and love to Adrian and Audrey. They can barely remember having to pay entry fees to events, purchase meals, pay for petrol or even holidays. The believers sacrificed not only to ensure they were keeping good company but to help them in their faltering steps following the Saviour.

But now both Audrey and Adrian were searching for the next

step in life. For Audrey, though, finding a career was amazingly simple – it found her! Her school, Perth Academy, had organised a serious of mock interviews with local businesses to help train pupils for future job interviews. Audrey had an interest in banking, as her older sister worked also in the bank, and Audrey wondered if this might be a suitable career for her. The manager of the local bank interviewed her and was so impressed that at the end of this mock interview he offered her a real job! Amazingly within a week she was being sought by another bank to come and join their staff – two job offers within two weeks. Audrey accepted the second offer and commenced her career in banking.

Getting to grips with banking seemed to be relatively simple for Audrey. In 1989 when she started work, the bank was still in the dark ages. Computers were rarities with each branch having only one. Cheque books were still printed in her tiny branch and the bank staff still knew the customers by name. Audrey was given the menial tasks to do, "You need more experience before you can face the customers," her supervisor said. She diligently applied herself to learning all about banking and quickly showed her capabilities to remember long strings of numbers. At her teller's position she could see onto the main street outside and watch if any customers were about to come in. As she spied the customer she entered from her own memory their account number and printed off a bank statement, so it was ready before they even asked for it. Today she still has an amazing memory for random numbers. She often talks in her sleep and has even sat bolt upright in bed and called out, "Next customer please," and then started to talk about financial services. When she heard the house number for her second house she was so delighted that it was number 25 that she said, "That's a lovely number! 25 it's so flexible, its square root is 5, and if you multiply it by 4 it comes to 100!" When the phone number was announced it was even more exciting, the first three numbers divided by the second three numbers came to the number 7, the perfect number.

Her banking career also became an extension of her quiet witness for her Saviour. Audrey never needed to preach; she lived the Christian life before her colleagues and simply spread the Gospel with her life. Occasionally she discovered some of her colleagues were Christians and the hand of fellowship and friendship was extended. "Come round to our house, we are having a barbeque," would be the invitation. A few would come, and despite the fact her first garden was smaller than most people's car, they would enjoy the barbeque and chat.

In the early 1990s banking in the UK was a serious career for dedicated professionals. For staff to make progress, there were years of exams to study for and the promising new starts were encouraged to sit these exams. Audrey was offered the opportunity to complete these exams, and her employer even allowed her some time off to attend college and study. Studying was never a problem, but fitting things into her increasingly busy life became a problem. She had strict rules, study until 9 pm, then put the books away and spend some time with Adrian. She decided that there would be no study on the night of the midweek Bible study and no study on a Sunday. This meant that when she got down to studying then she had to be serious at it. It also meant that she also had to go to the residential training centre in Edinburgh and learn about the loneliness of being a Christian in a worldly environment. While the others were content with evenings spent in a bar, Audrey was alone in a strange town, but content as she pondered what would Jesus do?

The bank exams also introduced her to a new source of contacts to speak to about her Saviour. Her radiant personality drew people to her and soon she was a friend, a colleague and then a taxi driver. Wherever her college friends needed a lift to, she was there! One day when driving back to college with her college friends, she stopped behind a car as it was turning right. The driver immediately behind wasn't paying attention and drove straight into the rear of Audrey's car. The car was heavily damaged, in fact it was an insurance write off, but thankfully Audrey and her friends seemed unhurt.

Audrey also had to face a period without Adrian as he headed off to University in Dundee. Their relationship was flourishing and she was going to miss Adrian during the week, but she could look forward to seeing him every weekend. University for Adrian, though, was an expensive business, and Audrey would regularly check the balance of his bank account. If she noted that there was any risk of being overdrawn, she would quickly transfer money from her bank account into his. Adrian was slow to understand the wonder of electronic funds transfer, "I just don't understand," he said, "the money never seems to run out!" Audrey was demonstrating her generosity in the face of apparent ignorance! Back in Perth, she had also been tasked with looking after Adrian's prize goldfish. This beautiful fish had been treasured by Adrian, but within a week of living with Audrey it was dead! Audrey phoned him and solemnly said, "I have some bad news, there has been a death in the family." Adrian waited for the terrible news. "Who was it?" he said. When Audrey broke the news, "It's your goldfish!" relief came, and then Audrey added, "I don't understand, it was doing somersaults and acrobatics, and then it was dead." The post mortem revealed that her hairspray had caused the equivalent of an oil slick over the water of the bowl and suffocated the fish. Audrey now prefers her fish with chips!

When Adrian entered his 2nd year at University, he wanted to purchase a car to use at University and at the weekend when he saw Audrey. He was offered a reasonably new car to purchase - a rather quirky little Fiat 126. The Fiat 126 had a 650cc engine, and it could travel along at a reasonable pace – if your ears could take it. It had many quirks including a heating system which connected directly to the exhaust pipe, causing noxious fumes to enter the car when the heating was turned on. The Fiat was truly tiny, with a rear engine and front storage area with barely room to store a soft bag.

The car was nicknamed Zacchaeus and Audrey and Adrian made many a happy trip in this little puddle jumper. The greatest challenge was running the leaders back to the Gospel Hall after they had been on the Sunday School bus. Audrey and Adrian were neat and compact but the two McGahie boys were both well over 6 feet tall and they always volunteered to go in the back. They bent their necks, curled their backs and crushed their legs in. These were fun times for them all. One evening after the Youth Fellowship Adrian couldn't find Zacchaeus. "Where is it?" he wondered. Just then his friends started roaring in laughter, "Look behind the bush," they said. Earlier the boys had quietly sneaked out of the house, picked up Adrian's car and moved it behind this large bush - a harmless prank that strengthened the friendship of this happy group.

The car came to the end of its life with the failure of its clutch. Adrian didn't have the money or the desire to fix it so he advertised it for sale. Three weeks passed with no enquiries, then out of the blue, a young couple phoned about it. Adrian told them about the car and its condition and said, "We even called it Zacchaeus after the Bible character." The lady replied, "Are you a Christian?" Adrian replied that he was, and the lady said that she and her husband had just been praying about it and this confirmed this was the car for them. The couple travelled from Aberdeen to Perth to purchase the car, and they even paid the same amount that Adrian had paid when he first purchased it! The oddest thing though, was the man was actually a helicopter pilot, driving some of the fastest and most versatile machines in the world, and now he was the proud owner of one of the slowest and possibly worst cars in history.

As Audrey and Adrian grew in their faith, they developed a burning desire to share more of the life saving message of Jesus Christ with the people they came in contact with. Adrian invited a university friend, Peter, to McDonald's for coffee and he began to witness to him. Peter had never heard anything like it before, and was curious at the zeal of his class friend, wondering if it was all real. "Why don't you come and hear Audrey's father preach in Dundee," invited Adrian. Peter agreed. John began to preach with his usual fervour and Peter was presented with a powerful sermon on true repentance. Peter wondered, "Is this real or is this just a sales pitch?" It was going to take a number of years before Peter realised that the Bible was true. They continued to invite Peter to Gospel services in the area surrounding Dundee. One evening Adrian was preaching in Tayport and Peter came to listen to his university friend. Immediately after the sermon, Peter headed back on his motorbike, but within 100 metres of the hall, Adrian spotted him on his knees at the side of the pavement. Adrian rejoiced, "Peter is getting saved!" but he was to be sadly disappointed – the chain on Peter's motorbike had snapped!

A few months after university was completed for them, Adrian's phone rang, "Hi, it's Peter. I'd like to come and see you on Saturday." Peter came through to Perth, but could barely hide his joy, "I've been saved, I've trusted in the Lord." For Adrian and Audrey, their prayers had been answered; the Lord had added another to His Kingdom.

At university, Adrian was able to organise a series of outreach meetings to his fellow students. He plucked up courage at the end of a lecture and with the lecturer's permission he addressed the 200 students, "Please come and hear a message from the Bible in the lecture theatre tonight." One of the girls who attended was deeply touched by the messages preached, and soon placed her faith in Christ. Years later, Adrian and Audrey sat listening to a missionary from Bolivia who told them of the new head teacher in their Christian school - it was the same girl who had been converted in Dundee. They rejoiced that God had not only saved her, but sent her to this far off corner of the world to serve Him.

When University was nearly finished for Adrian and the bank exams passed by Audrey, they started to discuss plans for marriage. Adrian wondered if this was God's will, and he sought to find what the scriptures said. One evening he got great peace, when he read, "Whoso findeth a wife findeth a good thing, and obtaineth favour of the LORD" (Proverbs 18:22). Adrian got down on one knee before Audrey and asked if she would marry him. She responded quickly and the excited young couple began to prepare for life together. The final hurdle for Adrian was asking John if he minded that he married his daughter. John was pleased to say yes, and they began to prepare for another happy day in the life of the Campbell family.

CHAPTER 5

Marriage

For Audrey and Adrian their engagement meant they had lots of things to sort out, especially with the date of their wedding set for the 30th September 1994. Adrian had just finished University and needed a permanent job. They would need to purchase a house and decide exactly where they would call home.

Obtaining a job for Adrian was an unusual process. He had been happy doing temporary jobs in an office near his parents' home, but one day when he returned home his father had decided to help him find a permanent job. "Son, I have left a job advert on your bed, you'll apply for it!" George Ferguson had left his son in no doubt what he needed to do! Adrian delayed but eventually sent in his CV, several weeks after the advert had first appeared in the paper, but strangely he got a call the next day inviting him for an interview. Turning up for the interview, he was applicant 138, but within 30 minutes the interviewer turned and said, "I have never done this before, but I am offering you the job right now." Adrian was delighted - a permanent job in a big company and with good prospects.

Audrey and Adrian then purchased a small house near Adrian's parents and quickly roped in volunteers from the Gospel Hall for its complete refurbishment. These young friends were delighted to help, and the neighbours watched daily as things took shape. Soon the garden was completed and the house itself was ready for the young couple to move into. Audrey had a real desire that her home would be used to help others, and soon she would be filling it with guests enjoying Christian hospitality.

With their wedding date fast approaching, they asked one of the close family friends, Arthur Pollard, if he would conduct the marriage ceremony. Arthur didn't just want to turn up and say a few words from a marriage book. He wanted the couple to study what the Bible taught about marriage. "Audrey, perhaps you can study Proverbs 31 and see what a woman is like in her home," resounded Arthur, "And Adrian will you examine the life of Abraham and Sarah." Arthur was pleased to set this task and even more pleased to discuss their findings from their study of the Bible. He didn't just ensure they were legally married, he continued for many years after their marriage to phone them, ask for their welfare and eventually help to lead them into a new service for God.

The wedding day came and everything went perfectly. Sarah was now seven and fulfilled the role of a beautiful flower girl, but she tried all day not to smile as her two front teeth had just fallen out. Peter Ferguson was the best man and as he gave his speech he pulled out of his pocket a set of false teeth and proudly handed them to Sarah - she could at least smile for the rest of the day. Adrian wondered how he could share his faith, without preaching at the wedding guests, so he stood up and started to tell about happy days growing up with his brothers in the family home, but then reminded everyone of the great joy in knowing another friend, one that "sticks closer than a brother", the Lord Jesus. Then he quoted a hymn. He could never have known its profound message for their lives:

> *"I do not know what lies ahead,*
> *The way I cannot see,*
> *But One stands near to be my guide,*
> *He'll show the way to me."*

They headed off to Cyprus for a two week honeymoon. The highlight of their holiday was visiting Israel to see that land where their Lord had walked. Getting into Israel was considerably more difficult than they had imagined. The tickets were booked in their married name, Mr & Mrs Ferguson, but their passports were still in the separate names, Ferguson and Campbell. Before they even left Cyprus, the Israeli security officer quizzed them about everyone they knew in Cyprus, where they had been and what their future plans were. Then they boarded the ship M.V. *Romantica*, probably the most inappropriately named ship ever. It had seen better days, and burst into flames and was scrapped just three years later. Waiting for them was an Israeli secret service agent, who was the best trained interrogator they had ever met. They had nothing to hide, but her questioning made them feel guilty, they couldn't wait for the questioning to be over. When the ship eventually docked in Israel, another interrogator was waiting for them, this time at gunpoint. The queues of buses were waiting to go, but every detail of their lives had to be examined before any bus could go. The sign rather ironically said, "Welcome to Israel!"

After the honeymoon, life back home in Perth settled into a happy routine of work, home life and involvement with Perth Gospel Hall. Adrian was put onto a management training course at work, and was asked to present something that interested him, in front of his fellow management trainees. "What will I speak about?" Adrian wondered, until he decided to share his faith in a most unusual way. He stood up with just a simple flip chart and asked the question, "Am I mad?" He gave the highlights: "I speak to a person I have never seen. I read a book that is thousands of years old. I live by laws that were written on stone tablets – am I mad?" The trainees gawped as the reality of the argument hit home, "You know me, and you know I am not mad," said Adrian as slowly it dawned on their minds that there was surely some truth in what he said.

Audrey and Adrian wondered how they could share the Bible with a number of the young boys who lived near their home. "Let's start a Boys' Bible Class," they concluded. Adrian recruited the boys and they sat down for a mixture of Bible teaching, food and games. As he began to speak the boys' faces revealed all, he could easily have been speaking in Chinese - they didn't understand a word of what he said! Next week it was back to the drawing board, "I'll make it really simple." So week after week Adrian and Audrey were starting to learn how to keep it simple with boys who knew almost nothing about the Bible. Some of these boys are now following the Saviour and preaching the Bible with vigour and fervour. Every week after the Boys' Class, the phone would ring, "Hello Bro, how did it go tonight?" It was Arthur Pollard returning from his Children's Club in Forfar. These five second phone calls were a hallmark of Arthur. He was so keen to pray intelligently about those serving the Lord, but with so many people to call he couldn't speak for long.

Audrey loved to show hospitality. They were very surprised to hear of the planned visit from an International famous religious leader. One of Audrey's neighbours was a publisher of Tibetan Buddhism books and she was always excited to tell of her latest thoughts about Buddhism. One day she came round to see Audrey and was all excited - the head of all Tibetan Buddhists is coming to the village, the world famous Dalai Lama. "Do you mind if I bring him round to see you?" What an unusual visitor - a man revered by some to be a god, followed by others as a politician and looked on by others as a great man of peace, and for some reason he was coming to Methven to visit the Fergusons. Audrey talked it over with Adrian. "What are we going to do? Will we give him a Gospel tract? Will he accept a cup of tea with us - does he take milk and sugar? Will he try to convert us to Buddhism?" Unfortunately the visitor never came, he must have been diverted onto other more pressing business, but Adrian and Audrey were learning that life together would bring to them many unusual experiences.

CHAPTER 6

LAM

The snow was just starting to lie on the ground as Audrey stared out of her window. It was December 1996. It had been a cold and wet month, the ground soaked with rain water and now the frost was making the land as hard as rock. A deep fear spread over her neighbours; they had experienced awful flooding in 1993 and were concerned that the mighty River Tay might flood their homes again. Her in-laws, George and Jean Ferguson, had endured the horror of over one metre of flood water rushing through their house and Audrey was concerned for their safety that night. The flood had been a trial, but the evacuation from their home and the mindless pilfering of their possessions had been depressing. Audrey could barely contemplate what sadness another flood would bring to the people of Perth.

She, however, had much to rejoice in! She had just learned that she was pregnant and she was starting to plan for the arrival of her first child. "There will be so much to do," she thought as she anticipated an exciting few months. But her joy was quickly forgotten as she suddenly started to feel unwell. First a slight chest pain, then mild breathlessness, and then the pain became more acute. Soon it became a struggle just to complete her daily tasks. It was impossible to sleep, so she stood and watched the crystal-like snow fall from the sky that evening. She wondered, "How many others are watching the snow fall this evening?" An appointment was made with the G.P., but he wasn't sympathetic: "Calm down, you're over-reacting; lots of people have chest infections and you're just one of them." He quickly scribbled a prescription for some antibiotics then off to see his next patient. Unconvinced of the diagnosis, the tears began to run down Audrey's cheeks. It was a searing pain. "How will I manage nine months like this?" She would soon realise that the pain and struggles were going to last far beyond the months of pregnancy.

Under normal circumstances a person with acute chest pain and increasing breathlessness would be given a standard X-ray to ensure nothing more sinister had occurred. As it was in the early days of pregnancy the physicians tried to delay exposure of the unborn child to radiation, so Audrey had to endure further days of pain and uncertainty. The antibiotics had no effect on her symptoms and she started another treatment cycle of further medicines, "Perhaps these will relieve you," suggested the Doctor. The pain and breathlessness, though, failed to lift and soon she could barely venture over her front door step. There were few options left but to do the X-rays and to see if any problem could be identified.

They immediately revealed a problem - one of her lungs had collapsed. "What an unfortunate coincidence," concluded the medics. The treatment to re-inflate the collapsed lung was an age old technique of inserting a tube into the chest cavity. Audrey was aware of the technique as she had read the exciting story of a British lady who experienced a collapsed lung on a Jumbo jet returning from Hong Kong. Without the drama of a 30,000 feet flight, Audrey grimaced in pain as the tube was inserted. The Doctors grinned, "You must be an athlete - your muscles were hard to pass the tube through!" She didn't feel much like athletics that day!

After only a few days in hospital, Audrey was back to good health and dashing around celebrating with her family and friends the news of the pregnancy and the adventure so far. Within a few days, however, the pain and breathlessness returned, and she was re-admitted to hospital for a second attempt to re-inflate the lung. The Doctors were puzzled, "How could her lung have collapsed again so quickly?" Her case started to gain the attention of the specialists. As the chest drain was being inserted, her muscles were to prove too much of a challenge for the first four doctors. One by one they tried to insert the drain and one by one they failed. Then a surgeon was called for and his experience shone through as he inserted it. Audrey just had to lie back and grimace with the pain as slowly her lung began to re-inflate again. Within a few days she was home again, hoping for a longer time before any further hospital visits.

With the lack of success in Perth at keeping Audrey's lungs inflated the medical staff started to plan for further treatment in Edinburgh. Her latest X-ray and scan had revealed that there were cysts over the top of her lung and further investigation was called for. With the February frost still hard on the ground, Audrey and Adrian reported to the hospital in Edinburgh where a new surgical procedure was to be attempted. That hospital has long since closed – it seemed the last place for modern surgery. Its decaying buildings with broken apparatus must have been a difficult environment for these medical experts to work in. The highly specialised surgeons explained the simplicity of the procedure. "We'll make a small incision and then using keyhole surgery attempt to seal the cysts by stapling them, making it impossible for them to leak again." The surgery commenced, but these specialists were faced with a challenge that they had never imagined. Inside Audrey's lung were hundreds of cysts - it would be impossible to staple them all. They hoped that by stapling a few large ones her condition would improve. It was hope without evidence! During the surgery a small biopsy was taken. This was to be a critical moment in the diagnosis of her condition. That night Audrey's bed was moved to a shared room, and wonderfully the lady that Audrey shared the room with was Freda, her friend from the Gospel Hall, who was also being examined for a serious lung condition. What joy they brought to each other as despite their illness the Lord was holding them in the palm of His hand.

As Audrey returned home to a measure of normal life, the pathologists were studying her lung tissue to try and conclude what the underlying condition was. Their expertise would be tested, as soon they would realise that Audrey's disease was of the utmost rarity. A few days later she was due for a routine clinic appointment. She had not expected any bad news, and simply hoped that as the pregnancy progressed her condition would improve. Her specialist, Dr Brown, greeted her and sat her down to break some shocking news. "Audrey, we have your results, and you have been diagnosed with an illness that affects one person in every million!" Audrey had heard Adrian say before "she was one in a million", but now there was at least evidence for it! Dr Brown continued, "Your disease has been identified as Lymphangioleiomyomatosis (LAM). It is not related to your pregnancy and I don't know what you will be like in five years' time." Audrey pondered, "What was he saying? Do I have less than five years to live?" The doctor explained more, but by now she was struggling to come to terms with his news and the rest went over her head. She thanked the doctor and then headed out to her car for a quiet moment of contemplation. "What does all this mean?" She was confused and perplexed by the suddenness of this life changing information.

Up in Pitlochry, Adrian was finishing his work and starting the journey home to Perth when his mobile phone rang. "Hello, I'm Dr Brown, Audrey's consultant; I have some news to tell you." Peter Brown spoke slowly and sympathetically as he explained the seriousness of Audrey's condition. Adrian was trying to think of things to say, "But you can treat it can't you?" he said. The Doctor replied, "There is little that we can do for her at present." The experience was almost surreal as a stranger was now explaining the fragility of his beloved wife's health, and somehow he now had to try and grasp the weight of the information presented.

As Adrian entered their little home, he rushed to Audrey to give her an arm of comfort and reassurance, "Darling what does all this mean?" Audrey tried to explain her understanding and Adrian tried to explain his. The confusion of that day would soon drive them to examine all the published information on the disease. The publications made grim reading, "Perhaps death in four years, perhaps sooner than that!" LAM is a lung disease which results in the excess growth of smooth muscle cells, causing airways to be obstructed and less able to absorb oxygen. LAM erodes lung function making it increasingly difficult for a sufferer to breathe. It is normally found in women of child-bearing age, hence manifesting itself during Audrey's pregnancy. The publications explained there was no known treatment, with lung transplantation the only possible therapy but even that had serious risks.

With few answers from the experts, she began to turn to the Great Physician for guidance for the future. She started, "Why me Lord?" but soon began to ask, "Lord mould me as You would want me to be." These became precious times of adjustment for Audrey, learning from her Saviour and getting a little glimpse of God's will for her life. Friends began to rally round and give helpful advice, and leave literature that brought great comfort. One of her friends gave her a book by Joni Erickson Tada to read. Joni had been a carefree teenager when a horrific diving accident left her a quadriplegic. Slowly Joni learned to trust in God to help her in her life. She learned to draw using a pen between her teeth. She used her voice to praise God in song, and addressed large crowds to tell them of the greatness of God. Audrey was greatly comforted that a lady with such an affliction had learned to serve God with such fervency. Audrey began to wonder how she could serve God despite her trial. Soon God would open up many paths for her to follow.

With the fresh dawning of the seriousness of her condition, she began to search out whether there were others who had the same condition. Her specialist remembered that when he was in training he had once met a lady with LAM, and that some early research was being undertaken in Nottingham. Audrey quickly contacted them, "Hello I have just been diagnosed with LAM; can you help me?" The friendly voice responded, "We have just started a new patient support group and we have contact with over 30 patients with LAM." Audrey was astounded, "Thirty others with the same illness, perhaps we can help each other!" Soon Audrey would become an integral part of the new LAM Action Charity which helps to finance research into cures for LAM and support those suffering from it. Audrey herself appreciated the help she received from LAM Action and the way she could discuss the disease with others who were passing through similar trials. She started to visit local ladies who had been diagnosed with it. One of them died before Audrey could establish a strong bond of friendship. It was a cruel disease which affected people in many different ways.

Back home, Audrey refused to lie down to her struggles and as soon as she was well enough, she donned her painting overalls and headed to Pitlochry to help paint the Faskally House Christian Centre. Three short days later, and she was facing the nightmare of another collapsed lung. She noted, "25th March 1997: Bad day – lung down." It was becoming difficult to cope with the cycle of illness, health and then illness again. She did not know that she was very soon to deteriorate to a life-critical situation.

Amidst all the struggles, there were exciting days. On the last day in March, she had the great news, "I'm feeling well today, and guess what! I felt the baby kick for the first time today." There was hope at the end of a dark tunnel, with the anticipated joy of a new baby.

With Audrey having a short period of improved health, Audrey and Adrian took the opportunity on 4th April to visit their friends the Sutherlands who had recently moved from Perth to Northern Ireland, and they didn't want to lose touch with these dear friends. Bill and Margaret had constantly showed an exceptional love for the young couple, despite the fact they themselves had experienced years of very poor health. They had often sat around the table and prayed, or as Adrian recalled, "they chatted with God". To the Sutherlands prayer was a wonderful conversation they enjoyed with their Lord. As the holiday progressed it became clear that Audrey's health was not improving in the way the Edinburgh specialists had hoped. Even a simple walk in the park with her Irish friends was too much for the normally active Audrey, "I'll just rest on this bench here." She knew that each day of the pregnancy was causing further deterioration in her disease due to increased hormone levels. She never contemplated termination, as she believed a child is a gift from God, and He makes no mistakes.

When Audrey returned home she attempted to throw herself back into the life of her large extended family. She attempted to play football with her nephew and niece, David and Katie, but she recorded in her diary, "...but stairs are still a killer". Normally football is played on the flat! The next day she was very breathless, struggling to run after another of her nieces. It was a big grief to her that a little child was able to outrun her - she should have been in her prime. Amidst this struggle, she opened her home to another friend, David Newell, who was so keen to see her after hearing of her diagnosis and plight. He came as a delightful house guest to bring cheer to Audrey and Adrian in this time of need.

The Tuesday after David's visit Audrey visited her consultant, for another check-up. The latest X-ray showed that her right lung had almost completely collapsed. David would have been horrified to know that Audrey had been hosting his visit with one lung collapsed. For her this collapse meant the familiar process of aspirating her lung again so it could re-inflate. As soon as the procedure was completed, she headed out of the hospital and drove herself home.

In was now late April 1997 and Adrian was busy in his job looking after computer systems in the North of Scotland. That evening he went to bed early as he had an important visit to a control centre in Dingwall, which meant a long drive and an early start. That night Audrey's pain returned and she slipped through to the spare room. She didn't want to disturb Adrian, the visit to Dingwall was important to him. She confided in her diary: "Thursday 24th April 1997, Gradually getting worse all day – unsure why lung should have gone down so quickly again. Overnight couldn't sleep – or even sit, perhaps the worst I've been ever. Beginning to panic as it is impossible to get a breath to even go to bathroom." When Adrian rose in the morning, he went through to see Audrey. She was in great pain. "I'll need to see the doctor again", she said, "I'll phone my mum in a few hours and she can take me over." Adrian headed north, but back in Perth Audrey was re-admitted to hospital. Her mother took her straight to Accident and Emergency, and an X-ray showed that both her lungs had collapsed. She was immediately put on oxygen and taken to have drains again placed in her sides. That day the grave reality of Audrey's condition was laid bare. The hospital staff commented, "You could have died - two collapsed lungs is a critical situation." Audrey was realising that life was very fragile, and that her health was far more critical than she had imagined. The consultant was very concerned now, and he phoned the City Hospital in Edinburgh to decide on the next course of action.

As April began to draw to a close, Audrey prepared her bag for the transfer to Edinburgh for further surgery. The days that lay ahead were soon to take on a magnitude that she had never expected. They would be long remembered as some of the most turbulent days in her life.

CHAPTER 7

Anna

Returning to hospital was becoming just another routine that Audrey was learning to endure. She sat as still as possible while the ambulance transferred her to the now familiar surroundings of the City Hospital in Edinburgh. The journey seemed to take a lifetime, as the ambulance weaved its way through the busy Edinburgh traffic. Each twist and turn caused pain for Audrey, and even more shortness of breath. She hoped that this time the treatment would be a success. In a moment of contemplation she paused and thought of her unborn child and the stress the baby could be under.

The consultant was anxiously waiting for his patient. Within minutes of the ambulance arriving, he began to chart out the options to Audrey. He considered the most beneficial treatment would be to put talcum powder into the chest cavity. This would irritate the lung and cause it to stick to the chest cavity in a technique called pleurodesis. The difficulty was that Audrey was now in the 24th week of her pregnancy and the general anaesthetic proposed, carried a risk for the unborn child. The consultant anaesthetist explained the difficulties of treatment; especially when pregnant and assured her that he would take special care.

Audrey, though, was feeling very much alone in hospital. She keenly felt this loneliness and was strangely unhappy all day. Adrian was working in Pitlochry during the day and he was committed to conducting the Boys' Bible Class in the evening. It would be impossible to come to Edinburgh during visiting hours. His phone calls brought little cheer - Audrey sounded very distant, she was in pain and her mind was ill at ease. She tried to sleep, but the pain was excruciating and she felt so downhearted.

After a restless night, the morning broke slowly and the busy routine of preparation for surgery began. Audrey complied with their instructions and sat obediently while all the medical records were cross checked again. For what seemed like the hundredth time, she repeated her date of birth and address. She wondered silently, "When will the treatment start?" but kept her frustrations to herself. At last the anaesthetist came. Audrey closed her eyes and fell into this induced state of sleep. The surgeon quickly got to work, putting the powder into the chest cavity surrounding the right lung.

Back in Pitlochry, Adrian was eagerly watching the clock. It ticked so slowly all that day, in fact for over seven months it had dragged miserably. After changing jobs in October 1996 he had gone through a period of deep unhappiness. The prospects in the new job were better, the computer systems were more complex, and even the pay was better, but somehow he felt he had made a terrible mistake. Self doubts plagued him and it became a struggle to find the motivation to adjust to the new job. At least he could comfort himself that the clock had never failed to reach 5pm each day! Sure enough that time came, and off he dashed to see his Audrey in Edinburgh.

The operation had gone smoothly and after only a short time in intensive care, she was returned to the open ward. Adrian was pleased to see Audrey looking so healthy. She had a good colour and despite the lingering effects of the anaesthetic, they spent a happy time together. He grasped her hand and said, "I love you darling." She smiled back in a tender and loving way. She was in no fit state for any conversation that evening, too drowsy to say much. The old fashioned bell rang, visiting time was over all too quickly, and they said their farewells. Adrian had another lonely journey home to what seemed just like any other house and not like the usual vibrant home.

For Audrey it was another disturbed night as her lung was adjusting to this artificial irritant and she felt strangely unwell. As the morning came, and the effects of the anaesthetic had lifted, she started to feel pain, like a stomach cramp, and immediately her concern was about her unborn child. "Please can you check my baby's heart beat?" she requested. The hospital staff very quickly arranged for a midwife from the Simpson's Maternity Hospital to come and attend to Audrey, and by 8:15am the heartbeat had been checked and all seemed well. Audrey though was not reassured. "Could you please arrange for me to get a scan?" The nurse replied, "We will phone over to Simpson's straight away." By 8:30am the pains were getting worse and two nurses stayed with Audrey, but within ten minutes Audrey could feel that the baby was going to be born.

Panic spread around the ward, and all the available doctors came to help. The specialised mobile team from Simpson's was called and one of the chest consultants took charge of Audrey's predicament. It was a most unusual situation, delivering a baby in an open ward, in a hospital that wasn't made for a baby being born, being presided over by a chest consultant giving instructions! Within a further 15 minutes, a little baby girl was born. She was taken away from Audrey, placed in an incubator and rushed by Police escort to the neonatal special care unit at the nearby Royal Infirmary (Simpson's Maternity Pavilion). Every second counted for this child. Audrey could only glance at the baby - she didn't even have time to find out if it was a boy or a girl. Within another 15 minutes, she too would be transferred to the Royal Infirmary.

Adrian was blissfully unaware of all the events taking place in Edinburgh, continuing his usual job fixing the control centre computer systems. He had been under a desk checking the cabling and was out of normal communication. Returning to his desk, his phone indicated a few missed calls, but then it rang again. On the phone was a doctor informing him of the birth of his first child. To Adrian this news was a shock. He knew about the weakness of premature babies and the risks of survival. That very day, one of his colleagues had already celebrated the birth of a new baby into his family, but now was no time for celebration for the Fergusons.

Within minutes of hearing the news, Adrian was on his way south towards Edinburgh. He called John and Anna and his own mother, and asked her to accompany him to see Audrey. The next phone call was to Arthur and Christine Pollard, "Please can you phone around the Christians and ask them to pray for us." A prayer chain was immediately started as word of this crisis spread.

As Adrian entered the hospital, like Audrey he didn't even know if their baby was a boy or a girl. He only knew the birth weight – 1 lb 7 ounces. By now Audrey was in Edinburgh Royal Infirmary, so on to a new location and quickly to her side. She was lying in a side room, heavily sedated, on oxygen and high dozes of pain killers. Adrian burst in, "Hello Darling," and he kissed her gently. He checked on Audrey's health but soon he could wait no longer, "Do we have a boy or a girl?" She replied, "I think it's a girl." Audrey, normally so precise and exact, wasn't entirely sure. She had glimpsed at the baby for only seconds and was now under sedation. With Audrey being herself quite unwell, there was no possible way that she could see her new baby at that time, she would just have to wait until the hospital thought it was possible. As a lovely gesture, the nurses sent over a photograph of the baby and a letter explaining the visiting protocol for the neonatal unit. They also said that they would be ready for Audrey and Adrian to see their baby in the evening. Audrey's mother, Anna and her sister Moira came through to sit with her at this anxious time.

Adrian could barely curb his enthusiasm for the visit to the neonatal unit. They had longed for a child, now they could celebrate their own very special baby. A porter wheeled Audrey slowly, with a chest drain and morphine drip on one side, an oxygen cylinder on the other, through the maze-like corridors of this large hospital. The Simpson's Maternity Pavilion was an austere mock Art Deco building spread over six floors. Despite the fact that over 6000 children are born there each year, it had a chilly atmosphere with little warmth or apparent happiness. At least the centre was named after one of Scotland's favourite sons, Sir James Simpson, the doctor accredited with discovering the anaesthetic qualities of chloroform. Sir James had also been a prominent Christian. Adrian and Audrey had frequently distributed one of his famous Gospel tracts, "My Substitute".

As the lift stopped at the sixth floor, Audrey and Adrian laid eyes on their child, for the first time together. It was an amazing experience as they stared at their tiny baby. She was small, yet so perfect, a real baby but one who weighed little more than a bag of sugar. The child was being fully ventilated, as premature babies' lungs are only partly formed and need assistance for a considerable period before they can breathe unaided. She was kept in a special incubator to keep her warm and to protect her from any infections. On her head was a beautiful blue hand-knitted hat and on her body were sensors to measure her heart beat, temperature and other essential data. Despite the joy of a new baby, Adrian and Audrey were deeply concerned about the long term survival of their precious bundle. So tiny a child has so little natural protection, and they simply prayed that God would spare her life.

As they returned to the Royal Infirmary, the topic of their baby's name came up. There could only be one name as far as Adrian was concerned, "It has to be Anna, it's the loveliest name for a girl." Audrey paused, it was a precious name in their family already, it was her mother's name and a middle name already used by three of her nieces. Audrey agreed, "Yes, Anna, but what about a middle name?" Adrian replied this time with the Psalmist's words, "Weeping may endure for a night, but joy cometh in the morning." "We should call her Anna Joy, she came in the morning and she will bring us great joy."

The excitement of Anna's arrival was very much tempered by the concern for her health. Audrey was heavily medicated for the pain of her lung surgery and in some ways she was less concerned than Adrian was. He worried about Anna, he worried about Audrey, and he was concerned about the rest of the Campbell and Ferguson families. He was concerned about what people thought about Anna's survival chances, and he was anxious at every comment by the medical team. Reporting back to people to give regular updates was painful and Adrian really struggled in these days. At every opportunity, he would pay a short visit to see Anna. He couldn't touch her but he could lovingly gaze at her.

Audrey was starting to feel a little stronger after the trauma of surgery and giving birth. On Friday 2nd May 1997, she wanted to see Anna again, and a porter took her back for a prolonged visit to see her treasured child. Audrey sat for two hours, watching, listening, praying, thinking - and overall just amazed that such a tiny child could ever live. She wondered about the law of the UK that permitted such children to be terminated in the womb. "How could this possibly be justified?" she thought.

The doctors could see the improvement in Audrey and decided now was the time to apply a sludge-based pleurodesis to her left lung. She was to be given only a local anaesthetic and into the tubing that had been used for the chest drains would be poured this solution. The pain would be almost unbearable for Audrey. She had experienced great pain before, now she just hoped that the morphine would deaden it enough.

Into the room came a nurse, who introduced himself as Alastair. He could tell by the cards and Audrey's Bible that she was a Christian and he began to share his faith with Audrey. His personality and love for Christ raised her spirits and she knew the Lord had sent someone to be a help to her. As he left, he said something she was so pleased to hear, "If you're feeling low, I'll come in and pray with you." Audrey realised that the hospital was expertly dealing with her body physically, but this nurse recognised the importance of her soul spiritually, willing to bring the spiritual cheer she needed.

It wasn't long before Audrey was back on her feet again, with a chest drain in one hand and oxygen in the other, but at least she could walk. Her brave efforts to exercise made her a celebrity in the ward. Her fellow patients watched her slow steps along the length of the ward and cheered her on. Most of these patients were retired people, having recently had open heart surgery. They had experienced their own traumas, but they often would stop and encourage Audrey, "You're doing great lass, keep it up." Audrey laughed, a young lady in her mid twenties being cheered on by these lively pensioners. A few months earlier she would have beaten any of them in a race - how things had changed in such a short time!

Monday 5th May 1997 was the day the Adrian and Audrey had dreaded. Anna was starting to deteriorate. It was a dreadful day. Audrey's hormones were beginning to return to normal after giving birth causing a deep sadness to pass over her, the "baby blues". When she went to visit Anna in the early afternoon, the paediatric consultant told her that a hole in Anna's lung had been found. Only time could tell if this would heal, and the only option was to medically paralyse her on her side. The likely cause was the ventilator. The very thing that was giving her breath had been too powerful for her tiny fragile lungs. Adrian arrived after another day at work, and Audrey was visibly upset, as she broke the news to Adrian. They sat sullen faced, discussing all that the consultant had said. There seemed little to cheer them. As the evening wore on, they turned to read a few verses from the Bible in Matthew 18:14, "Even so it is not the will of your Father which is in heaven, that one of these little ones should perish." They had never noticed this verse before and they wondered if it was a message of hope for them in the midst of seeming defeat. "Could it be that God doesn't want Anna to die?" they asked. As Adrian left to return home, with his mother as his loyal companion, he could barely hold in his feelings. He felt like a jar with so much crammed into it that it would explode at any moment. Jean Ferguson is always the sensitive type and knew well that Adrian needed space. Just a few minutes after leaving hospital, they stopped to get fuel for the car. Adrian could hardly hold in his emotions, trying to restrain the tears as he filled up with fuel and paid for it. The cashier must have been confused as Adrian paid up with tears running down his cheeks - surely paying for petrol cannot be so painful? He still feels a deep sense of emotion if he ever has cause to pass that same fuel station in Edinburgh. Painful memories do not go away quickly.

Tuesday arrived and Audrey felt a little stronger again. A steady stream of visitors was now coming to see her, to support her, to be with her and to pray for her. She was disappointed that although so many had travelled a long distance to Edinburgh, they still could not see Anna. The neonatal ward was a very tightly restricted environment and only very close family would be able to see Anna. In the evening, Adrian and Audrey returned to visit Anna, then spent the remainder of the evening with Audrey's sister Moira talking about how sure they were that Anna was going to be okay. Adrian laughed, "I might even write a book about the experience!" He would soon learn that many tears would be written into his book.

He returned to work again on the Wednesday but he could not concentrate. It was a very worrying time for them and he wondered, "Why did I come to work today?" In Edinburgh, Audrey was not having a good day again. She couldn't face going to see Anna on her own and she would have to wait patiently for Adrian. The medical staff had realised that Audrey should probably be nearer Anna, so they moved her from the main hospital to the maternity block. The well-meaning staff though put her bed next to that of a woman who had just had a healthy baby. This was too much for Audrey and her stoicism broke, she began to cry. The nurses moved her to a more private room.

As Adrian arrived in Edinburgh, Audrey's parents were waiting for him. Adrian was so pent up with cares that he blurted out, "I don't know how much more of this I can take." He felt at bursting point. He needed to share his emotions without upsetting Audrey. John agreed, it was awful; the anguish was breaking them too. As Audrey, Adrian and the Campbells entered the neonatal unit, a consultant was waiting for them. Adrian stood as this stranger whom he had never met before, nor had even known that he was caring for Anna, introduced himself.

The consultant began to speak, "We think there is no hope for Anna, she is slipping away. There is only one more thing we would like to try." Everyone agreed to let him try anything to save Anna. Adrian glanced at his watch and realised that it was time for the weekly prayer meeting in Perth Gospel Hall. His spirits were raised. He thought, "Wait to see what God will do as He answers the prayers of His people."

Tea and biscuits were brought into a quiet room for the two families. "John will you pray?" asked Adrian, but John couldn't pray that night. His own struggle with what was happening was too much. Adrian was able simply to say, "Thy will be done." Audrey's eldest sister Lorna had come to see Anna but she could never have known how sad the visit would be. Lorna had made a massive sacrifice to come to Edinburgh, and she felt guilty that now she had to return home to care for her own new baby.

The hours were drawing on and the nurses suggested that Audrey and Adrian should get some sleep. The Fergusons had learned that when faced with illness and suffering, one of the things you have to do is to grab some sleep when you can. There was little choice of where to sleep, but the hospital did their best. The room turned out to be a labour suite. Adrian had never been in one before, nor had Audrey, for Anna had been born in an open ward.

A labour ward is at best sparse, at worst clinical. Audrey was given a hospital bed to sleep on, but Adrian was given a birthing bed, which is designed to allow easy access to a baby as it is being born. It is not designed for a comfortable night's sleep as it splits into two! Adrian was just about to drop off to sleep when his legs dropped between the parts of the bed! Back to sleep for another minute then again the legs slipped and awake again! They laugh now at the ridiculous situation they were in, but even those few minutes of rest helped prepare them for the grief of the day ahead. They saw their little child teetering between life and death and wondered whether the morning would bring hope or desolation.

Audrey woke at 3am and said, "I just want to see my wee girl!" They made the short journey upstairs to the neonatal unit, and the latest gas exchange tests were good. "Perhaps there is hope," they thought. The little hope allowed them a few more hours' rest. But when 7am came the news was completely reversed. Anna was going quickly, there was no way back now. They returned to the neonatal unit, and screens were drawn around Anna's incubator to give some privacy. In the few short days of her life, neither Adrian nor Audrey had been able to hold Anna, but now in her dying hours they could hold her tiny weak body. Dressed in a little dress, Anna was gently lifted her out of the incubator into Audrey's arms. She was smaller than most dolls, but still in God's eyes "fearfully and wonderfully made". Her chest heaved as the ventilator struggled to give her the necessary breath to survive. It was heart breaking to see one so fragile struggle so much. Adrian took Anna and enjoyed the precious moments with her. Tears streamed down his face, but he no longer cared about others seeing him.

They knew it was now time for them to face the reality of the day. "Please can you stop the ventilator." It would have been cruel to prolong the artificial survival any longer. The medical staff removed the ventilator and left them alone with Anna. Audrey held onto Adrian's trembling hand. They had been a family, now they would be just a couple again. Within only a few minutes, Anna slipped peacefully into the presence of God. Their only child was no longer bound by human weakness. She was "with Christ, which is far better".

Audrey and Adrian wondered why they were now in Edinburgh. Anna was gone and Audrey was steadily improving. "Please can we go home," Audrey sighed. The hospital staff obliged by planning to transfer Audrey to Perth Royal Infirmary, but there were legal formalities to deal with first. Anna's birth had to be registered, but sadly her death had to be registered as well.

In the normal course of life, parents would have the joy of registering the birth of their children. It would then generally be the children who would have the sad responsibility of registering the death of their beloved parents. Both solemn responsibilities fell to Adrian that day. Dave Martin, ever a strength in days of sorrow, accompanied Adrian to the registrar. As Dave and Adrian walked through the bustling streets of Edinburgh to the Registrar's office, Adrian noted that for everyone else life was just moving on as normal. Passing by was a heavily pregnant woman, not long until she would be able with joy to hold her baby. Another lady was pushing a pram, her child was growing up, life was continuing for them. Adrian felt crushed and broken. "Why had Anna's life been cut so short?" he wondered. He was pleased that the question "why" did not plague him forever.

As Adrian entered the room, the registrar asked if he had come to register a birth or death. He simply replied both. The lady behind the desk was a consummate professional, she never batted an eyelid, simply moved on to complete the legal formalities. Then the tricky bit - payment! After days dashing back and forward to hospital, Adrian had almost forgotten the necessity of money. As long as there was petrol in the car and his mother had prepared some food for him, life had continued without thought of money. The fee was approximately £30. He knew that Dave would pay, but he knew it was his responsibility. Someone else should not pay for such a personal thing. He reached for his wallet but there was no cash in it! He then noticed thankfully that the Government had moved into the modern era and accepted plastic money. He swiped his card and paid the fee. He left with two pieces of paper. He had hoped that it would be only one.

As Dave and Adrian went back to the hospital, they were greeted by his parents who had travelled through from Perth. Adrian was saddened that his father would only see his granddaughter in death not in life. George was determined at least to see Anna, "Can I go along and see her?" he asked. The staff arranged that a few members of the family could go along to the room where Anna's body lay. Adrian, though, did not want to join them, "I'll just sit and wait instead." He sat and pondered, "Why would I want to see an empty shell? Anna's gone, only her body is left." He got peace that he would see Anna again in the reunion in heaven.

The ambulance for Perth arrived and Adrian and Audrey sat silently in the back during the wearisome journey back to Perth. Ambulances are not designed for conscious passengers and so the view through a tiny crack in the tinted windows gave only a miserable view of Edinburgh. Soon they drifted off to sleep, exhausted by the days they had gone through and flattened because they had no child to take home with them. Arriving back at Perth Royal Infirmary the staff welcomed Audrey and showed great sympathy for her predicament. As part of their caring role, the hospital sent in a nurse who had also been bereaved of her first child, and Audrey and the nurse discussed their experiences. The distinction however became clear for Audrey, as the scriptures show so clearly, "that ye sorrow not, even as others which have no hope" (1 Thessalonians 4:13). Their first taste of personal bereavement brought their trust in the Lord into focus, and they learned that even in tragedy believers have great hope.

The sad and solemn scene was transformed in the evening when the entire Campbell and Ferguson families and their children came up to see Audrey and Adrian in hospital. The 'two to a bed' visiting policy seemed to be dispensed with and the children clambered on to the bed to hug their "favourite" auntie. Adrian and Dave sneaked out and ordered some Chinese food, before smuggling it back into the hospital. Hospital food had never tasted so delicious!

As some comfort in these circumstances, at least there was no problem organising a funeral director. Peter Ferguson's friend was the local funeral director and he came and kindly made all the necessary arrangements. Adrian said, "Please, Bob, don't wear a black suit, I couldn't face that tonight." Bob's Christian grace shone through. He worked for a long established Perth business and had buried many of believers in Perth Gospel Hall who had died. Audrey and Adrian had often seen him conduct funerals and noted his healthy respect for the scriptures and hymn singing. He also gave them a pleasant surprise - they didn't charge for funerals for infants. The owners had experienced their own personal tragedy and they wanted to ensure others received support during this time. Every penny counted in these early days of their marriage and they had made no provision for a funeral.

Adrian wondered what to say to the many Christians at the Gospel Hall who had been such a support to them during these difficult days. He picked up his pen and wrote exactly what he was thinking:

"It is with deep sadness, that our little Anna Joy passed away early on Thursday morning.

We enjoyed eight wonderful days, when we could watch her, see her movements and even look into her eyes. We were so hopeful that she would live longer, that perhaps our house would be enlivened by the noise of a baby, but for us it was not to be.

During these difficult days, please continue to uphold us before the Lord in prayer. Audrey and I would appreciate this so much.

We will be having a family funeral for Anna on Tuesday, which will be a difficult day. Please feel free to visit us soon.

Christian love,

Adrian & Audrey."

The funeral was a private family one in the chapel of the Perth Funeral Directors. At the front of the room rested Anna's coffin, the smallest white coffin imaginable. Arthur Pollard, who only a few years earlier had conducted Audrey and Adrian's wedding, conducted the service, with the gentleness of Christ in such delicate circumstances.

The family gathered and sang tenderly:

"There's a home for little children
Above the bright blue sky,
Where Jesus reigns in glory,
A home of peace and joy
No home on earth is like it,
Nor can with it compare;
For everyone is happy
Nor could be happier there."

During the service, Peter Ferguson gave a touching tribute to the short life of Anna. As he fought back his own tears he rose and said, "... it is a great privilege to be able to say a few words about Anna. She was a beautiful little girl. She was so small yet so perfect and we loved her dearly.

"Anna was first of all, Adrian and Audrey's little daughter. It wasn't difficult to see how much they loved her. They were both doting parents. You could tell by the glow in Adrian and Audrey's faces, just how much they loved her.

"Anna entered our lives on the 30th of April and changed them forever. There will always be an Anna Joy, in both the Campbell and Ferguson families. She was not a temporary thing, but a full fledged family member who was loved and cared for by everyone in both families.

"To Adrian and Audrey she was a beautiful daughter. To John and Anna and Mum and Dad she was a granddaughter. To the aunts and uncles she was a niece and she was a cousin to the children in the family. What is so special is that she was loved and prayed for so much, by the whole family.

Three words spring to mind when I think about Anna's birth: Sudden, Surprise and Special.

Her birth was very sudden. She entered this world in only fifteen minutes, quite unexpectedly and without time for anyone to prepare for her arrival.

"She came as quite a surprise because she was four months early, being born at 24 weeks rather than the usual 40 weeks. She came as quite a surprise to us all, and even more so to Audrey and Adrian.

"She was also very special. She was not content to let a midwife deliver her. She had to have 3 or 4 consultants in attendance so that they could give her the greatest possible care at her birth. She was special because she was given every possible medical skill to help her in her little life.

"Anna must have been one of the few babies to be born at the City Hospital, where Audrey was receiving treatment. After her birth Anna was taken by flying squad to Simpson Memorial where she was cared for by the staff there. I am sure that Adrian and Audrey appreciate the care which the hospital staff in Edinburgh gave to Anna.

"My first sight of Anna was on a Polaroid photograph that Adrian carried around with him. I was mesmerized by the photo. I sat looking at the beautiful baby in the picture. She was so small and so perfect. She had long fingers and toes, with tiny fingers and toenails. I remember what the Psalmist said, 'Fearfully and wonderfully made'. We give God thanks, that as Creator, He allowed Audrey and Adrian to have Anna for this little time.

"Anna was beautiful: she really was. She had curly hair and when I saw her in the incubator, she was lifting her left arm and kicking all the time. Adrian remarked that she was going to pull out her tubes if she kept going like that. He also said she was a real "Anna Whizz". She was just like her father in this way – always on the move, never stopping for a minute.

"She seems to have been marked by speed. Speed at her birth and sadly, speed of life. It was also easy to see her strength, determination and courage. When I look at Audrey, it is obvious where she got that characteristic from. She was a real person who was determined to fight and hold onto her life for as long as she could.

"Anna lived for eight short days but she has enriched our lives in a marvellous way, and caused us to share in all of the circumstances which made her such a special gift of life.

"In closing, we can remember the words of David when he experienced the death of his baby boy: "I shall go to him, but he shall not return to me" (2 Samuel 12:23).

"David knew that one day he would be reunited with his son in Heaven. For Audrey and Adrian, there is the guarantee that one day they will be reunited with Anna in Heaven, to be forever with God."

As Peter sat down, the family paused in contemplation at those words. There is a great reunion ahead for all those who trusted in Christ. What a hope for the Christian!

As the indoor service concluded, the family travelled across Perth to the graveside. Bob the funeral director carried Anna's tiny coffin and placed it in position for the committal. Everyone paused for a moment for their private thoughts as Arthur prayed and read the scriptures. A few of the family members then came forward and took the cords attached to the tiny coffin. The time came for the cords to loosed and Anna's coffin was lowered into the ground. She was "sown in weakness" one day she would be "raised in power".

After the funeral, the family returned to John and Anna Campbell's house and within minutes, Audrey had her nieces and nephews clambering onto her knee. These young children couldn't understand grief but they understood love and were willing to share theirs with Audrey. She now had no natural children but she had many others who helped filled this large void.

The funeral of Anna brought a measure of closure for Adrian and Audrey, and it was now time to attempt to return to normal life. Slowly over weeks and months they would attempt to rebuild their shattered lives.

CHAPTER 8

A New Experience

After the death of Anna, Audrey and Adrian felt pretty flat. They shed many tears and had some very low and sad moments. It was hard for them to consider how they would be able to move on in life and rekindle their vigour. They felt desperately unqualified for the experiences they had passed through - they were still relatively young themselves. Friends and family rallied round, with meals, company and many kind offers of help. Some people brought advice, others brought books to read. Adrian sat and read some of the advice which they brought. He is normally very stubborn, but he started to listen to those who had experiences of coping with bereavement. One of the bits of advice that stuck in his mind was, "Don't make hasty decisions. Don't move homes, don't change jobs, and don't change your lifestyle and friends." He had been struck down with great sadness and this was reflected in every aspect of his life. It was hard for him to sit and watch Audrey in such poor health and hard to try and smile when inside he felt so sad. Dark clouds were hovering over him and he started to be concerned over Audrey. "Lord, help Audrey not to break down!" The stress that he had been under began to seem so small compared to the anguish Audrey would be feeling. They wondered how they would get through this trial.

Just a few weeks after the death of Anna, the Gospel Hall was having some special outreach meetings in a community centre on the edge of Perth. This was an area where they had conducted many happy years of children's outreach. The Good News Club there had closed, though, due to dwindling numbers and a very rowdy youth club which immediately followed it. It was hoped that if these meetings were a success perhaps the Good News Club could be started again.

The leaders of the Gospel Hall approached Adrian and asked if he would organise these meetings. The usual planning and prayer was undertaken. The Christians joyfully visited around the doors and a number of children promised to come. When the week started, however, the whole thing didn't really go too well – in fact only a handful of children came. The previous work had stopped and it was clear that it wasn't going to start again. This didn't seem too much like the boost Audrey and Adrian needed.

A few weeks later, David Harvey, one of Adrian and Audrey's friends, organised a few nights of Gospel meetings in his village, and asked if Adrian would preach for a few nights. He did his bit to serve the Lord but again, there was a void in their lives. The usual vitality seemed to have evaporated in the young couple's life for the moment.

Arthur Pollard noticed the sadness of the grieving couple and started to think of ways in which he could encourage them. He visited John and Anna Campbell to encourage them, and then he would visit George and Jean Ferguson taking lovely flowers to brighten the room and lift their spirits. He would phone Audrey and Adrian and ask them how they were feeling. As summer began to approach, Arthur had a new suggestion for Adrian and Audrey, "Why not come and help in our summer camp?" For many years Arthur had organised Christian Youth Camps, in fact in one sense Arthur was Tayside Christian Youth Camps, with everyone fondly calling them 'Arthur's Camp'. "Do you think we would manage?" they said. Arthur replied, "The Lord will help you."

Imagine the scene, two relatively inexperienced leaders, who had suffered a bereavement of their only child and who were facing a life threatening disease – hardly normal camp leader material! They signed up and went off for their first ever taste of a Christian camp. What a revelation that camp was to prove to them. Soon they could barely get enough of it!

The preacher was Ian Campbell, a person Audrey and Adrian had only met briefly once before in Perth. As soon as they arrived, Ian seemed to take an interest in them. The week was a powerful experience. For one of the first times in their lives the Fergusons were witnessing the Lord working directly before them. Young children were seeking the Lord and receiving salvation. This was genuine interest, not worked up by emotions, but the work of the Holy Spirit. Ian gave what he called, a "Heart to Heart Talk" – and during the week, whatever the children were doing, someone was telling "Heart to Heart Talks", imitating Ian's broad Newcastle accent.

On the final night, a little lad whom Adrian had been able to help during the week, came to the organiser Alistair Mathers and told him that he wanted to be saved. Alistair just came with the challenge of the old chorus, "Into my heart, into my heart, come into my heart Lord Jesus, come in today, come in to stay come into my heart Lord Jesus." The boy came from a tragic background of poverty, family imprisonment, and being passed to and fro between relatives, but that day the light of the Gospel was shining in his soul. To Adrian and Audrey it was yet another evidence that God had been working in the camp and with them in their lives.

The camp came to an end but their interest in camp work had only just been kindled. Here was an opportunity for them to serve the Lord on their doorstep, and be able to share their faith with children in a non threatening way. Soon they were recruiting children to come to camp, and leaders to assist in the camp. Within a few years Adrian was organising three camps a year and speaking at other camps. What had been a bewildering experience to face in their grief, became a work that God had fully equipped them for. Audrey and Adrian reflected, "We might not have our own children, but God is giving us hundreds of other children to care for!"

At the camp, Ian Campbell kept on asking the Fergusons to come and meet his wife, Bitten. She was from Norway and Ian described her like a Viking with actual horns growing on her head. After he had finished joking, he concluded, "She is the loveliest lady in the world and you have to come and meet her." On returning home, Ian sent a beautiful hand-drawn map and an invitation to come and meet Bitten. They could hardly refuse such a genuine invitation. This map became a treasure which Adrian kept in his car for years.

Just prior to visiting Ian and Bitten, Audrey had a week's holiday, which her sisters had planned in a caravan park near Berwick upon Tweed. Audrey headed off in the convoy of cars, and Adrian was left at home to finish another week's work before meeting her for the journey to Newcastle. Strangely for him, this quiet week became one of the hardest and saddest ones he could remember. For no apparent reason all the anguish and grief of the previous few months seemed to be released and he was plunged into a period of deep sorrow. Just coping with working and eating became a struggle. He was so sad and could hardly bear the strain of being alone without Audrey. The Friday came and Adrian hurried down to meet Audrey and her sisters. He could barely fight back the anguish anymore. He needed to be back with Audrey and find the comfort she must have been bringing him. In the struggles of life not only had they the Lord with them but they had each other. Within a few minutes of arriving at the caravan site, Adrian had been volunteered to sail the rowing boats, race the children and to do generally whatever uncles are meant to do. The sadness lifted and Adrian was relieved to be back again with those he loved.

The final stretch of the journey was made that evening so that they would arrive at the Campbells mid evening. In the car Audrey and Adrian started to discuss, "What will Bitten really be like? Is she really the loveliest lady in the world?" Following the map, mile by mile they were getting closer. Soon the very street name was in view and then the house, and with a deep breath, they rang the doorbell. Bounding out of the house came

Ian, with a smile that could swallow a whale, "Come in and meet Bitten!" So they crossed the threshold into a new experience of life, meeting a real live Viking! Within minutes, they knew that Ian's words had been true all along. Bitten was lovely in all her ways. Within just a few minutes, the two couples were sitting and touching upon the deep sorrows that had been experienced in the last few months. The tears began to flow as Ian and Bitten listened while the rawness of the loss of Anna was poured out. In that front room that evening an affinity was struck in tears which has continued since with many tears and many smiles. It was to prove to be a key friendship in the city of Newcastle. This would be a friendship that would become critical in desperate storms that were soon to arrive.

Later that evening the Campbell children returned from visiting a friend. Ben was 18 and Naomi was 14, and they had been looking forward to meeting this much talked about couple from Scotland. Adrian and Audrey wanted to see what the Campbells were really like in their home circumstances, to see how they dealt with the problems and blessings of family life. It was a very happy family home. Ian was a man of principles and a man with incredible determination. When he had been a little younger, he trained to run marathons. In the same manner as the great Eric Liddle, one of Scotland's most famous athletes, Ian would not run any marathon if it was staged on a Sunday. However, he had set his heart on running the route of one of the local marathons, so he devised a plan where he and his friend marked the route by leaving bottles of water strategically placed every few miles. Ian then started the Marathon, completely on his own, running mile after mile without company or pace-makers. At least he would get first place in this race! After 26 punishing miles the "race" was over and he had completed the course in barely a minute greater than 3 hours - quite a remarkable time over such a phenomenal distance.

The weekend was soon over, and some closure to the sad days which had passed came for Audrey and Adrian. It was now time to return to normal life and to serve their Lord in the days that lay ahead. Ian and Bitten had been with them at a cross roads in their lives, and now the Fergusons, like David Livingston of Africa, said they would go whatever way the Lord wanted them to go, as long as it was forward! They returned to their involvement in Sunday School, the Boys' Bible Class, and their growing interest in camp work was fanned. Opportunities to become involved in God's work were growing and they were finding much joy in serving their Lord together.

One of the new ventures was the commencement of mini-camps, a 24 or 48 hour break away from home in a Christian environment. Soon there were over thirty teenagers coming twice a year to these camps. It was a great opportunity to continue bringing the Word of God to the teens. Year by year the Lord added to the camps, with the mini-camps in autumn and spring 2010 having 95 people attending. The Lord was working, and wonderfully they kept hearing of stories of conversion to Christ, and young people setting their affections on the Saviour.

Camps though were not without problems especially for Audrey. A week of little sleep and strenuous activity was taking its toll, and soon she was struggling to cope with a whole camp. She adopted a new role which demanded time but less physical exertion, that of camp counsellor. She often sat and listened to the teens share their problems, or raised the spirits of a leader who was struggling with the week. New problems were continually appearing. Mobile phones changed from being the possession of the rich to be the possession of everyone. They developed into camera phones and then with video added. The concern of inappropriate photographs was raising its head. Christians must be "as wise as serpents and as harmless as doves". Then alcohol was spotted on a few campers, even rumours that drugs had been used by some - the Evil One was attacking the work of God. Wherever there is a work for God there is opposition. The hardest knock though was not from outside but from inside. Some Bible teachers began criticising, speaking about the errors of camps.

Audrey and Adrian prayed for God's guidance in this matter. As they puzzled it over, a wise confidante stated, "There will always be those that criticise your work for God - some would rather have you doing nothing than something. My advice is get on with it and get the work done." They were echoing the words of D L Moody the famous American Evangelist, when he was once told by an irate church lady, "Mr. Moody, I don't like the way you do your evangelism." In reply, Mr. Moody said, "I don't necessarily like all of it either, but it's the best way I know how. Tell me, how do you do it?" "Oh, I don't," was the reply. "Well," said Moody, "I like the way I'm doing it better than the way you're not doing it." What they were doing might not have been to everyone's taste, but with renewed confidence they simply pressed on with the work. A wonderful encouragement came later from someone who didn't feel able to assist in the camps, but they assured them that they would become prayer partners, supporting the work before the throne of God.

As well as the serious activities of camp, there were many funny and heart warming experiences that Adrian and Audrey would learn. One camp coincided with Adrian's birthday. The leaders covered his door with newspapers with a birthday card stuck in the middle. When they opened their door to go to the prayer meeting, they were greeted by the birthday card and the newspaper wall. On another evening, some of the lads were having a bit of fun in their room, which got out of control. One lad decided it would be fun to sit in the sink - he was over 14 stones in weight, and the sink fell off the wall. The pipes burst and water drowned the room.

Dressing up for "Hunt the Leaders" competition became an annual event. Audrey once dressed up as an artist, and painted landscapes in Pitlochry gardens. Although her oldest sister is an artist, Audrey makes no claims to such talent. Soon a crowd gathered and some tourists said, "Do you mind if we sit and watch you?" As she entertained the crowd with her talents, an onlooker was heard to say, "Look at that poor man, he must have had a terrible accident!" It was Adrian dressed head to toe in bandages, hobbling around the streets. The crowd would be sorely disappointed if they ever found out it was all a bit of camp fun!

Another year, Audrey dressed as an old lady and sat on a park bench and did her knitting. An elderly lady joined her, and they sat discussing knitting patterns, the elderly lady completely unaware that her companion was still in her twenties! After the campers had discovered Audrey's disguise, eventually the old lady realised that Audrey was not quite what she appeared to be and said, "I did think your nose was rather large." Audrey began to laugh, her latex nose wiggling in unison with her laughter.

As their experience of camp work grew, the Lord was preparing them for their next challenge. One morning Audrey was completing her household duties when the telephone rang. The message came as a complete shock to everyone. Arthur Pollard, the founder of the camp, had died very suddenly. He had been the very life blood of the camps and it seemed strangely fitting that he had died just outside Faskally House, the permanent camp premises.

Arthur had been a vital mentor to Adrian and Audrey and they felt his death very keenly. With Arthur's death, came new responsibilities for many of the leaders who had devoted themselves to camps. A small committee was formed to help organise future camps and Audrey and Adrian were able to open their house for the first discussion meeting. The new committee would help to continue the work long established by Arthur and his wife Christine.

At one of their most recent camps, Adrian looked around and noted an amazing array of leaders and helpers. The man who washed the dishes had recently been bereaved of his wife. One of the team leaders was a pensioner who was to take his wife to hospital the next week for a hip replacement. Two of the young leaders had just moved up from being campers at the senior camp. The cook was a Managing Director of a large company, and one couple had their new born baby with them! The Lord was using all kinds of different people to reach children for the Saviour. Adrian and Audrey were glad that they had become involved serving the Lord in this way.

CHAPTER 9

Deterioration

Once Audrey had left hospital after her surgery, her health slowly started to improve. By July 1997 she was able to play a gentle game of badminton with her nieces, she got renewed joy in cycling and was able to do lots of housework again. The improved weather also raised her spirits and she wrote in her diary, "Feeling quite good."

Ready for the next challenge, it was a short walk in the countryside up Craigie Hill. Gingerly climbing the slopes, Audrey enjoyed the feel of fresh air rushing into her lungs, and feeling braver, they pressed on further! At the hill top, she turned to Adrian and said, "I'm going to see if my legs still work." While he puzzled over this statement, off she sprinted down the hill as fast as her legs could carry her. He dashed after her, "Stop, stop!" But Audrey continued until she had no more breath in her lungs, collapsing onto the soft heather, but satisfied that her legs still did work!

As time went by, though, her health slowly deteriorated. This was not a surprise. When she was first diagnosed with LAM, the statistics had looked bleak, with perhaps only a few years left to live. Audrey refused to consider these bleak statistics and with a smile and her ever optimistic outlook on life she kept her spirits up. She had battled this disease for years, and she was not going to lie down to it now. It was, however, becoming increasingly difficult to smile in the face of the effort of simply trying to breath. Even the easiest of tasks was becoming a struggle, and sadly she was often seen slumped over the back of a chair, simply trying to get breath. The disease in her lungs was spreading making them increasingly ineffective at processing the air she breathed in.

One of the first sacrifices she had to make was her career. Since leaving school her banking work was well respected for accuracy, efficiency and knowledge. When the sales targets seemed unachievable, she just faced it, snatching success out of the jaws of defeat! She approached her manager and asked, "Could I reduce my work to four days a week?" Reluctant to lose her from the bank he agreed to reduced hours and even allowed her to do some work from home – but not to take the cash home with her at night!

The reduced hours gave her a day to recover after a busy Sunday in the Gospel Hall. Tuesday, though, came very quickly and soon she was serving the customers and greeting them with her happy persona. However, as the deterioration continued, some of the tasks of her job became impossible. She could no longer carry the heavy bags of coins; even the chairs at the teller's desk became heavy to move and hard for her to climb on and off. Again she approached her manager, "Could I reduce my work to three days a week?" With understanding, again her hours were reduced. This meant reduced pay, and yet again the Lord overruled and all that the Fergusons required was met by the goodness of God.

After a few years of three days a week working, and with her now requiring oxygen, she felt unable to continue in her career. It had been a real challenge with declining health to juggle a career, a home and her commitment to Christ and His people. Her work doctor knew the day had come. "Audrey, you're not fit for work anymore; you should apply for your occupational pension." For some people the thought of an early pension would be a delight but not for Audrey. "I like my independence," she said, hating the idea of being a charity case. "But it's actually your money," said Adrian, "you will have your own income and you can spend it as you wish." The bank prepared the documents and Audrey signed them. Within a few weeks, she became a pensioner while still in her early thirties! She now felt quite at home with the older ladies at the women's prayer group. "We're all pensioners now," she could joke!

One of the last activities she helped to organise with her colleagues in the bank was a charity event. It was an Olympic themed games challenge in the banking hall. Her colleagues turned the queue barrier into lanes for the banking families to race up and down. Adrian was keen to show his prowess at hockey and challenged one of the young banking staff to a race. With hockey stick in hand and the ball on the marble floor, he raced his young opponent, only to realise his hockey skills were far poorer than the lad's on his right. Audrey told Adrian afterwards, "Oh, he's also a part time professional footballer!" At least his opponent was a worthy victor! At the end of the evening, they had raised over £1000! Her colleague added, "And the bank will match our money." From this swansong for Audrey, she was pleased to be able to pass on £2000 to the LAM Action charity.

Living with disability had its benefits. Since she could no longer walk very far, the government disability scheme, Motability, provided Audrey with a brand new car. When she considered what car to purchase, in typical fashion she concluded it had to be a car with bootspace for a wheelchair and oxygen, and with seven seats so she could run children to the Sunday School. Each week her little cohort would be waiting for her. Audrey would play their favourite Christian CD, and the children would always arrive with a smile and a song. Some of them came from homes which knew little consistency or love. In the short time with them she tried to show consistent standards and the practical love of Christ. As her deterioration continued the children adjusted to her needs. They all began to volunteer to help her move the seats in the car. They also went faithfully to the other children's doors to ensure they were ready. It became a great team, with the older children showing love towards the younger ones. When Audrey no longer had the energy to pick up the children, they started to get the regular Sunday School bus, but sadly they soon stopped coming, missing the personal care she had shown them every week.

The state of Audrey's health meant it was becoming increasingly difficult for her to attend the camp leaders' prayer meeting upstairs in Faskally House. She would set off, 30 minutes before the time, to climb the stairs, resting as often as she required. "I won't be able to manage the prayer meetings again", Audrey said. Adrian had an idea, "We'll install a lift in Faskally House, and you'll manage to the prayer meeting." A few hours later, as prayer meeting time approached, the lift was ready. Adrian said, "Climb on my back, you're going to the prayer meeting." So she did get there. Every evening the Faskally Lift ensured that Audrey could spend time praying with the other leaders.

One holiday, Audrey and Adrian caught the ferry to Belgium. After a few days walking the streets of Bruges, Audrey's legs were fatigued and she suggested that they could hire a tandem to allow them to see some more of the countryside. They had never ridden a tandem before, but were willing to give it a try. After only a few minutes pedalling, Audrey got tired and took her feet off the pedals, resting them on the bicycle frame. As Adrian pedalled twice as hard, the locals began to shout to them, "Heh, she's not pedalling!" Adrian just smiled; he was just happy to go the extra mile for her. Back at the town centre, Audrey jumped off the bike and found an appealing park bench. Strangely for Adrian, he just could not go the tandem without the balance of Audrey – it became proof that they needed to stick together at all times.

As Audrey's disease continued to spread, she decided that it was now time for a wheelchair. For a young woman, this was a very difficult decision, but she would rather use it than have to give in and stay at home. She looked so well, but her lung X-rays were revealing a rapid deterioration. She had as little as 12% of her lung capacity left and simple tasks were becoming impossible. Using a wheelchair on holidays was fine - no one would recognise her, but at home it was an issue, not just for Audrey but Adrian as well. One Saturday, Audrey was determined to go to the Gospel Hall open air service. She got her wheelchair and waited for Adrian to push it. In one swift move, she had forced Adrian's hand and now they were using it among her own people.

Whenever Audrey used the wheelchair, Adrian insisted that those they dealt with always dealt with Audrey herself. He was determined that she would not be treated as incapable. They had experienced this arranging to view a new car. The salesman treated Audrey as if she was incapable of rational thought. She sighed, "There's nothing wrong with my brain, it's my lungs" - and promptly took her business elsewhere.

Another addition to her lifestyle was the use of oxygen. She had been concerned that she would become dependant on it once she started using it. The Doctor smiled, "You have been dependant on oxygen since the day you were born!" The only difference now was that the oxygen was more concentrated. She started with just a few small cylinders of oxygen every month. As she continued to deteriorate she started to carry oxygen cylinders in a little trolley when she went outside. People began to stare, but she was just delighted to be able to live as normal a life as possible. At night time, she had a machine which took in air and pumped out oxygen. This noisy machine was kept in the spare room, with a long tube running to a nasal cannula. Soon Audrey's inventiveness came to the fore: "If we close the door of the spare room and put the damp washing there, the heat will build up and dry the washing!" The whole room was a tumble dryer, with the National Health Service paying for the electricity! A later brilliant innovation was liquid oxygen, which had light refillable cylinders, allowing longer days away from home.

Audrey and Adrian were invited to a wedding, and now she was wondering how she could disguise her oxygen. Adrian said, "No one will mind," but she minded - she wanted to look her best. After a few minutes, she returned to Adrian and said, "Do you like the look?" He stared - she looked beautiful in her new outfit, but then he noticed even the oxygen bag was ready for the wedding with a floral display attached!

As part of keeping her general fitness as high as possible, Audrey enrolled in the pulmonary rehab class at the local hospital. Most of the class had been heavy smokers and were now suffering from chronic obstructive pulmonary disorder. Audrey became almost like one of the staff, showing others how to work the fitness equipment and setting a good example for all to follow. Unfortunately for Audrey the hospital was built on a hill with very limited car parking. The effort to get to the class eventually became greater than the class itself, and it became a real struggle for her to continue. To make matters worse, the disabled car parking spaces were abused by others with no disability, and she was often greeted with rudeness if she asked for the space. She was learning that not everyone is sympathetic to disability. One evening after a trip to the local supermarket, she returned to her car to find a rude note. "We have reported you to the council for abusing a disabled pass." Audrey began to cry; she was struggling with her little shopping bag, her oxygen cylinder and the distance to the car, now an unsympathetic note. She was no cheat and believed always in righteous dealings. In the morning she phoned the council to mention the note. They re-assured her that they would take no notice of the flawed misconceptions of some member of public, and apologised for her distress.

In April 2008, Audrey and Adrian had a few days' holiday in Newcastle with their friends Ian and Bitten. Ian was in the middle of a children's outreach and the Fergusons were going to be attending the meetings. After a pleasant trip to the beach, they started on the journey to the children's service. Adrian was driving, but had to stop behind a driver who was turning right. In his mirror he noticed that a van was approaching fast and had not seen his car in front. The van driver drove straight into the back of their car which contained at least ten oxygen cylinders, some full, others empty. Adrian panicked, "Would there be an explosion?" After checking that Audrey was okay, he escorted her to safety at the side of the road. She was sore, something had been damaged, and she too was concerned about the risk of explosion. The car engine would not turn off, the electronics had been damaged. Very quickly the ambulance and police arrived. As soon as they learned of Audrey's condition, she was strapped to a stretcher and taken to hospital for a full examination. Adrian asked the ambulance technician to bring some of the oxygen cylinders, but unfortunately in all the chaos, he brought the empty ones! Within just a few minutes of reaching the hospital, a man appeared whom the Fergusons had met only once before. Almost like an angel sent when needed, he introduced himself, "I'm Ken and I'm here to help you." He brought coffee, tea and biscuits, with cheer and help in a strange place. Thankfully the examinations found no serious damage. As they were being discharged, Ken said, "Just you come round to my place, I'll make dinner." Ken's wife had just died and he was himself still in mourning, but here he was willing to put himself out for others. As they parted Ken said, "Here is my card, call me if you ever need help." A stranger only a few hours earlier, here now was a man willing to help his fellow Christians in their difficulties. Adrian didn't realise it would only be a few more months until he would be calling on Ken again.

CHAPTER 10

False Alarms

As Audrey's health deteriorated, she entered another stage in her experience - the investigation about receiving a lung transplant. There was no cure to LAM. It was leading to certain death, but for the possibility of a lung transplant. Audrey had watched one of her fellow LAM sufferers endure the final stages of the disease and had witnessed her struggle for every breath. It was a distressing experience. Audrey was further saddened that her friend had made a principled decision to reject the transplant option, due to her Jehovah Witness beliefs. The Fergusons discussed the importance of correctly reading and interpreting the Bible, and how many had drawn the wrong conclusion with respect to blood transfusions. Audrey herself began to research the whole issue and to her surprise, the Christian monthly *Believer's Magazine* published a series of articles on transplants which became a great help to her. She said, "If I'm going to have a transplant, I'll need to be sure this is the Lord's will." For Audrey this was literally a life or death decision. As she prayed about it, the answer came in the words of Jeremiah 29:11, "For I know the plans I have for you, declares the Lord, plans to prosper you and not to harm you, plans to give you hope and a future." She took this as assurance that the transplant was part of that hope for the future.

Audrey's consultant in Perth soon concluded, "I think it's time to get you assessed for a transplant. I'll make the necessary arrangements with the centre in Newcastle." The assessment was a special three-day inpatient clinic to evaluate the patient's suitability for transplant and if it was immediately required. If it was deemed to be imminently necessary then the patient would go on the list which meant they could be called for transplant at any time.

Adrian and Audrey packed their bags and headed to the Freeman Hospital in the City of Newcastle. This was their first visit to Freeman's but it would certainly not be their last! Freeman's was a vast complex compared to the local Perth hospital, but the cardiothoracic centre was small and homely with just a few wards and consulting rooms. Audrey's height, weight, breathing capacity, lung function and gas exchange were all measured. The gas exchange test was the one that she dreaded most, as the blood had to be taken from arteries not veins. The needle would go under her skin, and then the doctor would turn it hoping to hit an artery, but often taking 3 or 4 attempts to hit the correct spot. The pain was searing. Audrey nearly passed out with it. The nurses promptly put her head back and her legs up, to get the blood running back to her head. Yet she reflected that these arteries are all part of God's wonderful design in creation, a kind of armour plated motorway for blood rushing to oxygenate the whole body. If they were easy to penetrate, countless millions would die when they accidently cut an artery. The pain she felt was a protection mechanism; God makes no mistakes in His creation.

After some recovery time, the next test was the 6 minute walk test. This was simply to see how far the patient could walk in six minutes and how low their oxygen saturation fell during exercise. Audrey was taken in a wheelchair to a cool back corridor of the hospital. On her finger was the pulse oximeter to measure her oxygen saturation, beside her was a physiotherapist encouraging her to really try hard, and behind her a technician to catch her if she had tried too hard. She gave her best attempt and completed the course without rest or undue stress. Her stamina was still fairly acceptable.

The next test was conducted overnight, where her breathing was monitored during her sleep. Audrey laughed, "Sleep! With the lights on, sirens blazing, buzzers ringing, nurses talking –

some sleep!" To compound matters, one of the ladies in the ward was suffering from dementia and thought Audrey was her nurse. Adrian came in bright and early in the morning with a spring in his step, but Audrey looked more bleary eyed, "Here goes for another day." The second day was filled with X-rays, further tests and reviews. In the morning the decision would be made.

The surgeon, consultants and nursing team discussed with Audrey their recommendations for the future. The surgeon said, "Audrey, we confirm that you are suitable for transplant but think you would have a better quality of life without the transplant at present. If you continue to deteriorate, you will need a transplant within just a few years." Adrian and Audrey considered this was good news and returned home to continue life as normal.

As time went on, the review assessments became more regular and eventually the day came when the decision of the medical team was, "Now is the time to be placed on the transplant list, for a single left lung." Audrey was shocked, "I have been too well to get a transplant, now I am too ill not to get a transplant." This was the fine balance that the hospital was constantly working on - when is the right time? The Fergusons knew that their time was in God's hand, and their future was only as the Lord permitted. They just rested in God that day.

The news of being on the transplant list soon sank in, and lifestyle changes had to be made. Now Audrey could never be away from her mobile phone, never switched off, never out of signal area. Before going on holiday she would study the mobile phone coverage map, to ensure that a strong signal could be obtained. Adrian made arrangements with his work to cancel all further travel until after Audrey's transplant. Invitations to conduct Bible teaching were made with a caveat that they could be cancelled with little notice. Contingency plans had to be made for every activity they were engaged in. A new addition to their lives and car became the ready packed hospital suitcase.

In a single suitcase, were packed enough clothing and toiletries to help Audrey through her transplant and recovery, and enough to ensure Adrian had emergency provisions. Wherever the Fergusons went the suitcase travelled with them.

Audrey turned to her diary and began to write a very frank account of what might lie ahead. "I get very varied responses from people when I say I am on the Transplant List - some think it is wonderful, almost like I'm going to the dentist to get a false tooth, and others are shocked, clearly concerned about my future. What is the reality? Well, transplant is a very risky operation and about 20% will not survive the operation - however, that means 80% will! It is something that the medical people will only consider as an absolutely last resort. The reason for this is that there can be so many complications afterwards and you have to take anti-rejection drugs for the rest of your life to stop your body rejecting the organ. One patient told me she started off on 60 tablets a day - I'd better get better at swallowing tablets!! That of course will reduce with time, but my immune system will always be lowered by these tablets, making me more likely to catch infections.

"Having said all that, though, the benefits should outweigh the disadvantages. I really look forward to being able to take a deep breath, run up the stairs, and even do the housework; and to be free of the oxygen which has been my constant companion recently. There should be an immediate difference to my breathing capacity and quality of life (once I am over the pain of the operation!). How long does the new lung last? Well, the average figure they give is 8 years, however, some have lived 17 years with their new lung and that's what I am anticipating! - positive thinking always goes a long way!"

The first call from Newcastle came in the middle of the night. The Fergusons were in a deep sleep when the home phone began to ring. Like most families when the phone rings at an unusual time, they assume that someone has died. Adrian

Jock Campbell being presented with an RNLI award
(immediately behind man receiving hand shake, on left).

"The six girls"
From left to right: Audrey, Moira, Hazel, Ruth, Lorna and Mum - Anna.

Wedding Day September 30th 1994, with Arthur Pollard.

Adrian & Audrey with Lois, Laura and Peter Ferguson, 1997.

Audrey at Haggerston Castle in 1997 with her sister Moira and Sarah, Katie, Rachel, Darren and David.

Adrian as a climbing frame for the family in 1998.
Clockwise from top, Sarah, Darren, Rachel, Katie & David.

Adrian & Audrey on holiday together in 2004.

Formal photograph of Adrian & Audrey in 2004
for their tenth wedding anniversary.

Audrey with Emma, Katie and Moira in Holland, October 2005.

Audrey with Ian, Bitten and Naomi Campbell, April 2006.

Sponsored cycle organised by Audrey's nieces, November 2006.

Adrian and Audrey with fund raising cheque, September 2007.

Audrey with Daisy at Esther McKay's wedding, July 2008.

Waiting for the train from Battle to London, August 2008.

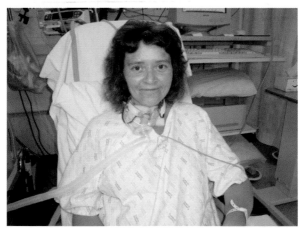
Last day in Intensive Care, 13th September 2008.

The family gathering to celebrate Audrey's return home after transplant, October 2008.

The West Highland Way walkers who raised nearly £10,000
for LAM Action, with Audrey in the centre, April 2009.

Family gathering for Moira's birthday. John and Anna 4th from left.

jumped out of bed and answered the phone as if he had been waiting for the call, "Hello Adrian speaking." The quiet voice at the far end was whispering, they were probably calling from home and didn't want to disturb their own children. She began to speak, "Hello it's Freeman's hospital here, I'm calling to ask, how is Audrey?" Adrian turned around to check Audrey was safely tucked up in bed, sound asleep, "Pretty well I think." Adrian was puzzling, why phone to check on Audrey at 3am. The nurse continued, "There is a possibility that a set of lungs may be available, please can you come down to Newcastle?" Adrian passed the phone to Audrey and started to get himself ready for the long drive. As he went to his bathroom, he began to shake like a child, wondering what was going on. Until now the possibility of a transplant and all the risks were just a theory to them. He tried to steady himself, "I don't want Audrey to see that I'm worried." There had been no rehearsal for this storm they were passing through. This was another step on the steep learning curve in their walk with God.

As the journey to Newcastle commenced, they sat silently, thinking things over on the long journey south. No scriptures came to comfort, or words of comfort that others had passed on, and it was too early in the morning to speak to others in the family. As they passed Dunbar, the words of the old hymn began to resound in their minds and voices,

> Kept, safely kept;
> My fears away are swept;
> In weakness to my God I cling,
> Though foes be strong I calmly sing,
> Kept, safely kept.

This was exactly the kind of comfort they required, to know their weakness, yet to know that God was their strength. The only problem was that the first verse was all that they could remember, so the journey had to be made singing repeatedly the only verse they knew. William Blane, a fellow Scotsman, had written these verses over a hundred years before transplants were practised, but they were just the appropriate words for their present experience.

In the dawning light of Newcastle, soon they learned that their journey was in vain. The lungs of the donor had been examined and were deemed unsuitable for transplant. So it was back to their car to begin the drive home again. After a few more hours sleep, Adrian was at work trying to carry on with normality. This was to become a regular experience, nights in Newcastle and days at work.

One of the things that occupied Audrey during these days of deterioration was fundraising for LAM Action, the UK based LAM charity. Audrey spotted another way to raise funds, "I'll enter Adrian in a 10K race, and he can ask for charity donations." Adrian agreed, although he had never run as far as that before. He had always joked, "I've got short legs, I'm built for sprinting not jogging". He refused to don any Lycra, but put on his old T-shirt and shorts and started running before breakfast every morning. The first few weeks were a daunting affair, but soon he was clocking up the miles and getting nearer the target distance. But the week before the race, he damaged one of his leg muscles. His training was over, and he hoped he would be able to run through the pain on the race day.

Saturday 11th September 2007 came, and over 500 runners gathered at the start line for "Running the Race". The elite athletes were at the front, the medium runners in the middle and Adrian at the back! The sun came out - the weather was exceptional for a late summer day in Scotland. The gun fired and they were off. Adrian started plodding away, overtaking a few, and being overtaken by many. After 4K, his feet started to go numb. "I'm not stopping now", he said, and pressed on, "I've got a lot of money to raise for LAM Action." As the finishing line was coming into view, the crowds began to cheer and he made a dramatic sprint for the finish. Like a race horse just out of the blocks, he sped past the stragglers and crossed the finish line with an amazing burst of energy. He finished in

54 minutes, a time which even he was pleased at - and his feet recovered quickly! Audrey counted the sponsor sheet - over £1500 raised for LAM Action, one of the biggest donations of 2007.

Audrey began to reflect on some of the Bible examples of running a race and the patience required. She began to write in her diary, Heb 12:1 "Wherefore seeing we also are compassed about with so great a cloud of witnesses, let us lay aside every weight, and the sin which doth so easily beset us, and let us run with patience the race that is set before us". "The runners on Saturday carried nothing extra with them - not even their mobile phones! They cast off anything which could hold them back. We need to be the same in our Christian lives, casting off anything (even if legitimate) which will hold us back from serving the Lord as we should."

Audrey must have been in a very creative spirit, as her diary entries went into overdrive. She recorded these on a Christian website to help others in their needs.

"You might wonder how the disease affects me on a day-to-day basis. Well, there is no doubt that it has changed my life dramatically. The main area is breathlessness. For those of you with medical training my FEV1 level is 0.45 ltrs (about 15% of predicted) and lung volume about 25% (I think!) This does make the very smallest of things quite difficult. I could probably walk about 50 metres on a good day before stopping and this would be with no wind and flat! It means the daily routine of showering and dressing etc needs some careful planning. It is all possible as long as there is plenty of time and lots of stops to regain breath. This has all become the norm for me and I'm quite happy as long as I know where the perimeters are. The perimeters have been coming in and in as the years have gone on, so I've had plenty of time to adjust gradually to these changes. It's not until you look at others of your age doing things that the reality hits you of what you should be able to do. I remember looking in awe and wonder at the camp leaders this year as they ran on 4-5 hours sleep sometimes, ran about all day in the various activities and still looked great at the end of the day! It really was amazing!

"Having said this though, I would say I enjoy life very much. There is so much to rejoice in and be grateful for - all the material blessings and we have absolutely everything we need, a wonderful loving and caring husband, Christian fellowship, lots of supporting family and friends and most of all salvation. This life is only 'as a vapour which appeareth for a little time and then vanisheth away' James ch4 v14, but what a hope we have for eternity! This is the great hope for every Christian and if we really believe the Lord could come back at any moment, it takes away the worry about the future - it's all in His hands anyway!

"I have found it more helpful to think about what I can do rather than what I can't do. Yes, I could go down the line of how much I miss - being able to play tennis which I enjoyed or long walks in the countryside, but this would not be helpful for me. I rather congratulate myself on what I have been able to do that day. It may be that I can manage to walk around Tesco with my oxygen one day instead of using the mobility scooter, so I will rejoice in that.

"I think for all of us it is important to keep mind and body as healthy as possible, and that way we function more efficiently. After leaving work due to my health I was very concerned with keeping my brain from slowing down. I began to learn to play the piano - something I had wanted to do for years and was too busy, so now I can sit down and practise my piano! I also began a computer course which keeps the old grey matter stretched as well as my pulmonary rehab class.

"Another thing I think is important too, is to keep mixing with friends and pushing yourself to do the things which are important to you. I have spoken to some patients and they feel like they cannot communicate with others on the same level as their illness has isolated them. In my experience my friends and family do want to know how I am but it is important too that we don't speak about our problems all the time - mixing more means we have more things to talk about and our life is far more interesting.

"Feeling sorry for yourself - well it's one feeling which wants to keep popping back up but is the absolutely worst thing for us! Normally I can put this to one side, but maybe once a month I allow myself to wallow for maybe half an hour before sending these feelings packing once more - they do us no good at all and we should always be looking for the Lord's help to be rid of these feelings."

Back from the excitement of the race, Adrian and Audrey settled back to normal life, waiting at the end of a telephone line. The weather soon changed, the sun fell lower in the sky and the rain returned. After another false alarm, they were returning home from Newcastle. The rain was falling as heavy as they had seen for years, and the moisture had reduced visibility and caused flooding over the roads. Peering through their misty windscreen, they could see the flickering light of something on the road ahead. Adrian couldn't work out what it was. He braked hard - mercifully just in the nick of time. Ahead of them was a puddle over 50 metres wide and flowing like a river across the main A1 trunk road. If their car had hit that puddle at normal speed the conclusion could have been fatal. They were shaken and anxious, but the Lord had preserved them.

As the calls became more frequent, Audrey started to share these on her internet diary. In October 2007, she wrote: "Another night on the roller coaster! Just to let you know I had another transplant call last night. The call came in about 9.15pm and my heart missed a beat again when they said it was Freeman's Hospital. This time they had a single left lung, which was perfect for me, but the downside was it was being offered to other centres first. They had to get me down to Newcastle in case the others who had priority didn't want it, and time was at a premium.

"We set off pretty soon after the call - on the road again to Newcastle after just arriving home on Monday night following a weekend's holiday there! We received a call from the co-ordinator just at the Forth Road Bridge to say they had now taken the lung out and it was infected. There is no way they would put an infected lung into you as they bring down your immune system completely after the operation and you would have nothing to fight the infection with.

"What was our reaction? - well one of resignation I suppose. I try not to get too uptight when we are going and therefore I don't feel too deflated when it doesn't go ahead. We just turned in to McDonald's and had a cheeseburger meal - who cares about the calories!"

In the midst of these experiences they continued to get a verse from the Bible that spoke directly to them. Audrey noted, "Jeremiah 29:11 'For I know the plans I have for you, declares the LORD, plans to prosper you and not to harm you, plans to give you hope and a future.' This is a verse that has comforted me and the Lord seems to bring it before me each time I am called. It was given to me on a gift first of all, and then appeared constantly in a book I was reading. One occasion I said to Adrian, 'I didn't get my verse this time,' and he said the night before he had been registering for a Christian software package and it brought up a verse to show it working and what verse was it? – Jeremiah 29:11. The Lord has amazing ways!" This verse continued to appear every time there was a false alarm - a call, a text message, an e-mail or letter came with this verse on it. One night when tidying a drawer at home, Adrian pulled out a card from his parents from 1994, and the verse was Jeremiah 29:11. Years before the experience they were passing through, the Lord had assured them of a plan made for them.

As autumn turned into winter, the rain stopped, but an iron hard frost came. On one of the coldest nights of the year, the phone ran at 4am. It was Freeman's. The conversation between the nurse and Audrey was very prolonged and Adrian started to make preparations for the journey. He pulled on some clothes and went out to defrost the car. The car was covered with ice and he scraped the car windscreens both inside and outside. After nearly 20 minutes, he returned inside to hear the end of the phone call, "Sorry but we cannot take you tonight." For once he was furious. "I'm absolutely freezing, I scraped the car and it is all in vain. I wouldn't have minded even driving to Newcastle after the effort I've made." But he soon calmed down, realising this was yet another trial to pass through.

One of the more humorous incidents was when Ian Campbell came to stay with the Fergusons for a week. He had come to conduct some children's services in Perth and had just arrived from his home in Newcastle. Ian and Adrian went to the Gospel Hall to unload his children's props. As Audrey waited at home, Freeman's hospital called and an ambulance was sent to take Audrey to Newcastle. Ian and Adrian were returning to Methven when Audrey phoned, "I've had another call and an ambulance will be with me in five minutes." Ian pressed his accelerator pedal and they sped back to the Ferguson home. Just as they crossed the threshold, the ambulance arrived. The driver came straight into the house and grabbed the suitcase from the front hallway. Ian shouted, "Stop, that's my suitcase!" Adrian and Audrey began to laugh, "Your clothes wouldn't be much help to us!"

The brevity of life began to be imprinted more regularly on Audrey's mind. She began to write, "From 80 to 78 Lammies. We have had rather sad news this last month. We lost one patient about a month ago (I didn't really know her, but sad all the same). On Tuesday morning though, another patient died who I was quite friendly with. I have met her at LAM conferences and she wrote very regularly on the patient chat line that I am involved in. We have so much in common with our disease and because it is such a small community we feel like we know each other quite well. I was very sad as she was only 40 and leaves behind a husband and two young daughters (youngest only 5). She was diagnosed with the disease 5 years ago and was only recently assessed for transplant. She had a terrible time though with chest infections and I guess this time her lungs decided they could take no more and gave in. It brings the reality of how fragile life is very much home to me. I know that my lungs are not in good shape, but I believe I am being kept so well because of all the prayers of the saints. I have not had one chest infection and that is quite a record for a LAM patient." Audrey hoped others would see the great need of donor organs and would commit themselves to being on the organ donor register.

Despite Audrey's positive approach to life, the number of false alarms was becoming a big concern, "Will a set of lungs become available in time?" The Christians in Perth could see her predicament and they began to draw closer to bring words of comfort. One of the older men looked at Audrey and said, "I think the seventh call will be the one that is for you. Seven is the perfect number in scripture; it will be perfect for you!" Audrey and Adrian counted the calls - they were rapidly approaching the seventh.

CHAPTER 11

Transplant

In August 2008, Adrian and Audrey packed their suitcases for another of their epic tours of Britain. Despite Audrey's deterioration they had managed to visit the extremities of the UK and Europe enjoying many memorable holidays. One year they visited the farthest north of Scotland, reaching the outpost of John O'Groats. A few months later they reached the other extreme at Land's End in Cornwall. The visitor centre there presents certificates for those who have covered the journey between each extremity of the UK. Audrey approached the counter and asked, "We have covered the distance, can we have a certificate please?" The reply was, "How long did it take you?" "Four months!" The man behind the counter raised his eyebrows, "And how did you do it, did you walk, or cycle?" She replied, "No, we just used our car!" His shoulders sunk, as he realised that Audrey's cross country expedition, whilst gallant, probably fell outside the category of a major achievement.

The Ferguson's choice for 2008 was the historic town of Battle, site of the famous Battle of Hastings of 1066. Battle was a full 502 miles from their village of Methven. In the busy summer traffic this would be a minimum of 8 hours driving, a mammoth effort for someone so ill, but Audrey was determined to have another happy summer holiday. The car was loaded with all the usual holiday goods, clothes, snacks, books, DVD's and oxygen cylinders! These oxygen cylinders had just become part of normal life and they were a visible reminder of the damage that LAM was doing to her lungs.

The little wooden lodge in Battle was in an ideal location overlooking the rolling countryside with views out to the sea, but one difficulty was the few steps up from the lodge to reach the car. For Audrey these few steps were a further struggle every time there was a trip out in the car. There was no possibility of pushing the wheelchair into the lodge, the ground was too steep. So she had to muster the willpower to continually push herself in her struggle against breathlessness. On the Sunday the trip out was to meet Christians at Marine Hall in Eastbourne. Though it was a small congregation, they had a big heart and immediately befriended Adrian and Audrey and showered them with kindness. "Come for a meal," they insisted, "meet us for ice cream," "stay longer," "come again," all said with genuine love and care. Audrey wondered how they could help this group of kind Christians. She suggested, "Can we help with the Air Show outreach?" They had printed thousands of beautiful postcards with photographs of planes and a Bible verse and challenge on the reverse, and they needed help to distribute them. Audrey sat in her wheelchair holding the pile as Adrian darted around the people giving out the postcards. Although she could only give out a few herself she was supporting the efforts of these eager Christians to reach out in their community.

On the final evening of their holiday, one of the younger couples invited them to their home for a farewell "Pudding Party". They had expected only a few friends, but they soon found visitors had travelled for many miles to enjoy each others' company, to eat delicious food and to meet these visitors from Scotland. It was a truly memorable occasion especially for Audrey as the friends wanted to get to know the real Audrey, not the young woman who was now dependant on oxygen cylinders for her vital breath.

The joyful days of the holiday were over, but as she was struggling with her ever increasing breathlessness Audrey said these sad but timely words, "This will be our last holiday as I am, I just can't manage another one." The travelling, the movement in and out of the wheelchair, the different beds and temperatures were all proving to be too much for her. As they sat contemplating the reality of what she had said, the impact was so vast that few words were exchanged on the journey home. The many miles were filled with thoughts about the future.

The future in many ways had always been an issue for Audrey. Her deterioration in one sense had been slow. Adjustments had been made at a daily level and coping strategies were readily invented. The possibility of a life cut short was always kept as a future problem. But the future was now becoming closer to the present. Her breathing statistics now reflected the true extent of deterioration - with only 12% lung capacity left, there was nothing in reserve. She was now at the stage where every deep breath was accompanied by a large surge in her shoulders. Her posture was often slumped as she sat down desperate for air to enter her lungs. The reality had dawned that if a cure or transplant did not come soon, Adrian and Audrey's future together might be brief.

The holidaymakers arrived home late on Saturday evening, emptied the car, including the transplant emergency clothes bags, and rested to get ready for reuniting with friends and family on Sunday. It was spent sharing stories about the exciting times of the holiday and the new friends made in Eastbourne. One of Audrey's nieces had been sick but she came down from her bed especially to see her special aunt again and to get a bit of tender care. The role of favourite aunt was one that was unquestionably Audrey's.

Monday was back to work for Adrian, determined to catch up on the work missed in the past two weeks. He waded through the paper work, fault listings and e-mails, working on right past his usual finishing time. There was just enough time for a quick meal and then out again to attend the Bible Study at the Gospel Hall. The Fergusons had rushed to the service early, unusually for them, to set out the chairs in the temporary hall being used as a Gospel Hall. The old Gospel Hall had been sold and a new site purchased to allow a new one to be opened. At this in-between stage the church was like Old Testament pilgrims, meeting in various locations over the year, travelling light and not quite knowing who they would meet!

Within minutes of entering the hall, Audrey's phone rang. It was Freeman's Hospital in Newcastle, enquiring if she was well enough to come down for a potential transplant. The constant phone calls from Freeman's had become very much part of their lives. This was expected to be their eighth false alarm! Audrey waited outside the hall for her Mother. "Mum, I've had another call from Newcastle; do you want to come with us?" Her mother couldn't come, "I think I better stay and look after your cat as she has been left in the house." Audrey replied, "I guess as usual we will probably be back home tomorrow." Audrey's Dad had just stepped onto a plane to Singapore for a month-long preaching tour. Anna had stayed at home so that she would be free to help Audrey in case the call for a transplant came.

The long miles to Newcastle were familiar. Soon the sun was setting and as darkness fell the bright lights of Newcastle began to shine as a beacon of hope in the midst of a great trial of affliction. Adrian parked the car and gently pushed Audrey in her wheelchair along the corridors of Freeman's hospital. This place had been a daunting sight on the first day that they had laid eyes on it for the lung transplant assessment, but now it was a place which offered the possibility of a life saving event.

They patiently waited for news of the potential transplant. The minutes turned into hours and eventually at about 1am the news came from the medical team that the donor's lung was unsuitable. The prospect of another long journey home in the darkness held little appeal, but just as they considered getting a nap before the journey the medics asked them to wait as there was a possibility of another donor in the morning. For Audrey, she would have to try and get some sleep in the all too familiar surroundings of a hospital ward, but for Adrian it was a blanket and a seat in the patient's dayroom. These seats seemed to be designed deliberately to make you as uncomfortable as possible, forcing you to sit bolt upright. The prospect of falling asleep in one of these chairs also leads to the possibility of falling out of the chair straight onto the hard floor. He resourcefully pulled two chairs together and bent his body into a U shape, trying to get some modicum of comfort. It must have been a strange sight for the morning staff to find him lying in this contorted position, snoring, still in his shirt and tie from the anticipated Bible Study a distant 12 hours earlier. With sleep now over, he enquired about Audrey and got the news that the transplant was very likely to go ahead.

Adrian rushed to be with Audrey and, like two excited youngsters waiting for Christmas, they began to discuss the possibility of the transplant. Very quickly the full medical team was assembled and the probability of a transplant turned to reality - the operation was to go ahead. In this most stressful of circumstances a great sense of peace came upon them. God had brought them this far, in a few hours a new life would begin for them. There was never a fear that things might not quite turn out as planned. These surgeons had over 1400 transplants to their record and Audrey believed they would be guided by the Great Physician.

It was at 11.35 hrs, on Tuesday 19th August 2008, when Adrian said his goodbye to Audrey, "I'll see you in just a short time, everything will be okay." She smiled back, the anaesthetic already making her feel drowsy. She held Adrian's hand and they responded to each other, "I love you." Adrian, ever in a hurry, noted the time and remembered that he would need to allow at least 5 hours for the surgery to go ahead and initial recovery to happen. As surgery commenced, he prayed that there would be success. It wasn't an impressively crafted prayer, just a heartfelt sigh, looking for a loving God to answer it. He knew that God can take our sighs and answer them.

Adrian's priority now was to get a change of clothes and a hot bath. The irony was that for over a year and a half, they hadn't travelled a mile without the transplant case, but that was now back home in Methven, emptied, with all their holiday clothes. The local ASDA superstore provided something to wear for the next few days. Audrey normally chooses his clothes, often laying out what matched so that he would not make a fashion faux pas, but now he was free to make his own mistakes. Amazing what you can purchase for £10, he thought, why does Audrey spend so much! He headed back to the hospital room which he had been allowed to use, shaved and bathed and put on his new clothes. "Audrey will be impressed when she sees them", he thought, as he cast his eye over his stop watch. The hours were slowly moving on. No word from the hospital yet. The waiting continued.

Early evening came, and Adrian made his way over to the intensive care ward, where he was told to wait until Audrey had been fully put into her post-operative position. There was no news other than that the transplant had happened; nothing was said about any concerns. The door was opened and Adrian could visit her. There she lay, helpless on a hospital bed, ventilated, anesthetised, unable to move, a radically different sight from even a few hours ago. Into her arm and neck were lines of drugs and fluids. A single line transfusing blood went into an artery - strangely it was her own blood which had been harvested during the surgery. For one strange moment Adrian cast his mind back to the radio play "The Blood Donor" and laughed when the blood donor received his own blood back. Audrey was having her very own blood donor moment.

In the intensive care ward, there is one nurse to each patient. Audrey's nurse was a male nurse who had seen hundreds of transplant patient. "How is Audrey?" Adrian asked. He paused and began to read the statistics: her breathing function was low, yet the ventilation device was on maximum. It was a very bad sign. Adrian looking for hope and comfort asked, "Is this normal?" "No," was the reply, it was not normal, Audrey was seriously ill, something was wrong with the transplanted lung.

Adrian tenderly stroked her face and hands; her face was strangely warm, he dreaded ever having to find Audrey with a cold brow. Her normally radiant face was marked with contentment. It was an assurance to Adrian that at least she looked comfortable in her present predicament. The brief minutes were over and Adrian had to leave Audrey to the care of the expert medical team.

Returning to the day room to wait and make some phone calls, he reached down for his newspaper but it was gone. A visitor dressed in casual clothes and pink croc shoes sat contentedly reading his paper. "Next she will be doing my crossword!" he thought, nothing was sacred in hospital.

Then it was the first of a regular diet of meals in the hospital restaurant. The time still moved so slowly. He consumed the chicken with peppers, and his apple crumble, and sat back wondering why, as usual, had he eaten too much? At least it passed some time! Waiting was a painful experience for Adrian; he preferred living life at full steam ahead. In his pocket were two mobile phones and the messages constantly appeared on the screen, sending greetings and prayers from all over the country. It was exhausting keeping up with communications, and eventually the off buttons were pressed.

At 20.20 hrs Adrian returned to the ICU to see Audrey. Even since the last visit, there had been deterioration; the medics were getting concerned. Her ventilation was on at 100% but her oxygen saturation was dropping and was now only 85%. The experts decided to give Audrey a further internal examination to see if there was any damage or fluid in the new lungs. The next update was due in about 30 minutes.

Adrian left the ICU only 15 minutes after entering, now bewildered and confused. He turned to his God and began to pray again. Alone in that hospital he had the assurance that many others were praying for Audrey at that precise moment. Seldom had Adrian been alone before, he had been usually supported by family in trials and especially by Audrey. Now she was unable to help, his family were 3 hours away, even John was in a different continent. At that moment he felt an incredible weakness, any bravado gone, even prayers seemed to stop. He needed someone to be with him as soon as possible.

Adrian pulled out Ken's number. He was the friend who had helped him in their car crash earlier in the year. Sadly there was no answer. Only later did he learn that this gentleman was only five minutes away from Freeman's hospital that evening. Next he was going to call his dear friends Ian and Bitten, but they were out and expecting visitors later in the evening. Wiping away the tears and sobbing he wondered what to do next. He began to scroll through his telephone address book. As he reached the "M's" he wondered why he had been so slow to remember - a dear friend Jim McMaster lived just 15 minutes away from the hospital, and Jim knew plenty about sitting with people in crisis. Adrian pressed the call button and Jim answered. There was no small talk, Adrian just said, "Jim will you come and sit with me, I can't cope on my own." Jim said, "Sit tight, I'll be with you in 15 minutes." To Adrian it seemed like the longest 15 minutes in history. "Where is Jim?" he wondered, pacing the car park in the fading light of that mid August day.

The friendship with Jim had been long lasting one. At the Bible Study weeks and weekends in Perth, Jim was a regular speaker and encourager of the younger people. He was 100% Scottish and proud of it. He had a great sense of humour and infectious enthusiasm for God and His people. Despite many years living in England, Jim looked and sounded like he had just come out of the Scottish glens, with his busy moustache particularly reminding the youths of a Highland cow roaming the rugged Perthshire countryside. He was even known to dress his son in a kilt for his visits to Perth - how could he ever forget his roots!

Jim and his wife Janet suffered a number of crisis moments in their own experience, with health concerns and deep family troubles, for example when a consultant broke the news that perhaps their only son would go blind. They felt crushed with the news, "How can it be?" they wondered, "Why us?" In despondency they turned to their Lord and their spirits were lifted and hope given for the future. Soon the news came that the illness was less serious than initially envisaged and their son's eyesight would be normal. They rejoiced that God was able to help in troubled days. This trial to their faith would enable them to help others experiencing deep trials.

It was just after 9pm when Jim arrived. He greeted Adrian with his trademark rib crushing hug. "Come on; let's get a coffee," he said, as he marched Adrian off in the direction of the hospital canteen. The only place open was the doctor's restaurant. This was not an insurmountable problem to Jim as this rugged Scotsman also has an air of authority, and very quickly, tea and coffee was being served to them both. As they sat holding the scalding cups, Jim started to ask Adrian what was happening. Adrian was like an opened book pouring out his troubles into Jim's ears, he was so glad that someone could share them. For Adrian the loneliness of not having Audrey to confide in was heart wrenching. They had passed through all their previous trials together. Now they were passing through this seemingly insurmountable trial in one sense very much apart.

Adrian's phone began to ring; the caller was Professor John Dark, one of the UK's most eminent surgeons, and Head of transplant surgery at Freeman's hospital. Professor Dark had been at home resting when the medical team had called him to help. Audrey's condition was rapidly deteriorating, and they enquired if he could do anything to help. His strong voice came booming over the phone, "I'm coming in to see what we can do. Perhaps there is a twist in the lung, or a leakage." The Professor's words were not laced with hope, merely facts that this bleak situation may get even more bleak. The team had already begun to examine Audrey with their scopes to see if they could get any indication of the problem.

Adrian was dizzy with the rapidity of the events, "How could it be, that Audrey could now be taken from me - she was so vibrant just a few hours ago?" he thought. Jim knew that circumstances were rapidly beginning to spiral out of man's hands. It was time to leave our cares with God. Jim began to pray and chat, and phone and pray, taking charge of "Mission Control" and becoming the vital link to Audrey's many praying friends and family.

Back in Perth, the family had a measure of celebration at the good news of Audrey's transplant. Her sister had just returned with her family after a fun filled holiday in the USA. They were jet lagged and exhausted after flight delays and time changes, and joked with Anna that they will take her to Newcastle any day but not today! In the midst of their celebration, Jim called, "I think you should come down - tonight." With these words ringing in their ears, within minutes Anna, Ruth and Dave were on their way south on a mercy dash.

Even further north, Robert and Jenny Thompson were visiting friends in the City of Aberdeen. Robert and Jenny had been friends both through Perth Gospel Hall and the Tayside Christian Youth Camps, and they had shown a particular interest in Audrey's condition. In August 2008, Robert had just commenced his training as a hospital anaesthetist in Freeman's and they had set up home in Newcastle. Adrian called him to discuss Audrey's predicament. Robert replied, "We're on our way down to sit with you." Adrian protested but Robert simply said, "We're coming!"

Across the River Tyne on the outskirts of Sunderland, Ian and Bitten Campbell had just returned home, fixed a quick supper for guests, then dashed out to sit with Adrian in the hospital. They came into the tiny waiting room and hugged Adrian to show their continual love for him. Ian could barely pray, he loved Audrey and now the crisis was a real trauma for him as well. Adrian wondered what kind of friendship he had ever introduced them into. It had commenced with streams of tears and now the tears had become rivers.

The waiting was agony for the little group, soon to be joined by Robert and Jenny after their lengthy journey. Time seemed to move on so slowly, with so little information to report and endless speculation in the waiting room. Robert sat quietly, he knew the risk of transplants and that intensive care has as many defeats as it does have victories. Whenever a medical term or procedure was mentioned, he patiently explained it and why this was being considered.

Just after midnight Professor Dark came into the waiting room to inform them about his next step. He was surprised at the swelling numbers in the room, "Where were they all from?" he wondered. Adrian encouraged the Professor to speak openly - they were all part of the "family". He spoke slowly and carefully, his face had the look of a defeated man. "We are going to take Audrey back into theatre tonight, I will open her up and see if there is any problem with the way the transplant has been completed. The risks are serious, the way things are progressing she may even die during surgery, but there is nothing more we can do, and we are willing to do what we can. Sadly we don't have long; I have two further transplants to complete this night." His face had said it all, he was lost for options and he wondered if there was really anything he could do. The surgery was scheduled for little more than 30 minutes time, yet Anna, Dave and Ruth were still travelling from Perth. Could they make it in time to see Audrey?

Jim phoned, "Where are you now?" but the response was that the Perth travellers were still nearly an hour away. Adrian was deeply distressed; he was desperate for Anna to see her youngest daughter Audrey alive. The time moved slowly for the travellers yet quickly for those in the waiting room. Would Anna not make it in time to see Audrey? "Bitten, will you come instead?" said Adrian. Bitten took hold of Adrian and with a trembling lip and tear filled eyes she entered the intensive care ward. Bitten approached the bed where Audrey lay helpless, kept alive by the puffs of the ventilator and the infusions of drugs. Bitten looked beyond the pipe work and saw her friend Audrey, "Hello Audrey, it's Bitten here, I've come to see you." Bitten lovingly stroked Audrey's face and told her of her love for her. There wasn't much more that Bitten could say; she was just willing to "weep with those that weep".

Jim's phone rang, it was Dave, they were reaching the entrance to Freeman's hospital. "Can you meet us and show us where to go?". Jim left the waiting room and stood outside the hospital waiting for his friends from Perth. When they arrived, Jim said little - he felt it was not his place to convey too much news, but his glum face betrayed the sense of agony he was experiencing. As Anna entered the room, her assumption was that Audrey had gone. She ran to Adrian and held him, "Why Audrey?" her youngest child, so very dear to her heart. Adrian could read her face and wanted to share that there was still some hope. "Let me speak for a minute, I'll just tell you exactly what's happening." Adrian began to repeat the words of the surgeon and to share that Audrey's life was hanging by a thread. "At this very moment she is in surgery, but there may not be anything they can do."

As the atmosphere in the now overcrowded room darkened, Jim began to pray, pouring out his soul to God. Adrian and Dave joined in prayer, praying not "platform" prayers but simply cries to a God who loves to answer prayer. Adrian lifted his head and asked, "Have you got a Bible, Jim, could you read us a few verses." Jim dashed to his car for his Bible and returned to read. His choice of scriptures was about a lovely day in Heaven, about the beauty of the place, and the Lord who occupies heaven's throne, all from the book of Revelation. Adrian could understand Jim's idea, but as far as he was concerned, the end was not yet, these scriptures could be fulfilled another day. Adrian spoke up, "Jim, will you read us Psalm 23." He began to read, "The Lord is my Shepherd, I shall not want." The room was united in sobbing, everyone present had followed the Shepherd - now what was the Shepherd going to do in this circumstance? "Though I walk through the valley of the shadow of death, I will fear no evil; for Thou art with me, Thy rod and Thy staff they comfort me." Never in all their experience had the valley of the shadow of death been as close as it was in that room that early morning.

News from theatre had dried up but the praying continued. Jim seemed to be the only one now capable of praying and his prayers seemed to rise to a new intensity. He so naturally moved off his chair onto his knees on the hospital floor. This was a man pleading with his God about a friend who meant the world to him. Jim had long ago stopped saying prayers; he was conversing with one whom he knew as his Father, and was pleading for a precious child.

The time was almost 3am, Jim was on his knees and the family and friends had bowed heads in prayer. Just then ominous footsteps were heard in the silence of the hospital corridor. It was Professor Dark. He so respectfully waited for Jim to finish his prayer. This time the face of this renowned surgeon was entirely different. Instead of the look of utter defeat, his face shone. He began to speak, "We have examined Audrey carefully and we cannot find anything wrong with the surgery. We think for some unknown reason, the transplanted lung had developed a condition like an injury. We think that it might be possible to very slowly nurse Audrey back to health. It will take a long time, but there is a possibility she will live." Tears of joy, like he had never experienced before, poured out of Adrian's eyes, then he spoke, "Take as long as you like, we have all the time in the world, just give us back Audrey." The atmosphere in the room was one of absolute triumph, God had answered when medicine felt defeated. Never had the family been at a prayer meeting like this before.

The Professor then explained that Audrey was to be put on an innovative device called a Novolung which would remove the carbon dioxide from her blood and help her lung to rest. This device had been in Freeman's hospital for only a year and was to be one of the critical factors in Audrey's survival.

After the agony and ecstasy, it was time now for some rest to regain strength for the days ahead. The friends departed and agreed to meet for some breakfast at 9am. Dave and Adrian retreated to their room. Adrian read a few verses of scripture to give further comfort, and then closed his eyes to grab any sleep he could. Within minutes his body had shutdown, he was fast asleep.

The most dreadful noise entered the room at 5am - it was Adrian's phone ringing most fearfully. He had spent the last 12 years covering 24 hour emergency response in his employment, but never had there been a more concerning phone call. He grabbed the phone, "What's wrong, what's wrong?" The answer was, "This is the intensive care department, I'm phoning to tell you that Audrey is getting on fine on the Novolung." Adrian thanked the well meaning nurse, but he now was suffering heart irregularities and dripping in sweat. He puzzled at why they had phoned to tell him good news? He crawled back into bed, but sleep was almost gone. There would be few normal nights' sleep for many long weeks.

Circumstances back in Perth, immediately following the transplant, had not been any easier for friends and family. The Gospel Hall friends had convened an emergency prayer meeting. They loved Audrey and were devastated at the prospect of losing this dear Christian. The believers gathered in one of the local homes; it was not time for elaborate prayers, but earnest intercession in this critical situation. In the homes of Audrey's nieces and nephews, there was also great concern and anguish. If the phone rang, they all ran to answer or listen in. Katie Martin refused to go to bed and puzzling what to do, Katie and her sister Emma got their white board pen and wrote on their board, "Pray for Audrey". These words summarised the best thing anyone could do for Audrey, pray for her. It had been a night when many wrestled with God, from the very youngest to the most mature. The truth of the old hymn shone through:

> *Before the throne of God above*
> *I have a strong and perfect plea.*
> *A great High Priest whose Name is Love*
> *Who ever lives and pleads for me.*
> *My name is graven on His hands,*
> *My name is written on His heart.*
> *I know that while in Heaven He stands*
> *No tongue can bid me thence depart.*

As the morning broke in Newcastle, it was not with peace and jubilation that Adrian arose. The storm was not over, but perhaps the first of the great rolling waves had passed and the boat was still intact. He rejoiced at any glimmer of hope before them. The medical experts were still puzzled at the events surrounding Audrey's transplant and they began to draw a conclusion about what may have happened. They thought that she had suffered a "Reperfusion injury". One of the mysteries of transplants is that a working lung can be taken and transplanted then become a damaged lung. It becomes ineffective, stiff, almost as it had been ill-treated, bruised and battered. Reperfusion injury is one of the major causes of early death after lung transplantation, yet Audrey had survived. Her friends prayed that she would continue to beat the depressing medical statistics. The medical care she had received was, perhaps, the finest in the world. Her surgeons and clinicians had been major contributors to academic research in the very area of reperfusion injury. They had charted the treatments that had been beneficial and monitored the exact dosage of the few treatments available. With trust in God and confidence in the medical professionals, the spirits of all who waited for news of Audrey were being lifted. It was to be the beginning of her long road to recovery.

CHAPTER 12

ICU - The Critical Stage

As the sun rose on August 20th 2008, Adrian wondered whether Audrey could survive the day. The family assembled for breakfast just before 9am and tried to help each other adjust to the day and night they had all passed through. They specially thought about John who had just reached Singapore when he received a phone call about Audrey's plight. It had been real challenge for Moira to try and contact him, with the time difference, the many preaching arrangements and the language barrier all slowing down contact. Eventually John was located and he was listening, "Dad, it's Moira, Audrey has had her transplant and she is really ill." John was stunned by the news, so far from home. For years John and Anna had cancelled holidays or preaching visits, knowing that Audrey could get her transplant at any time. The friends in Singapore and Malaysia, though, had been particularly persuasive and persistent in their invitations to John, so eventually he agreed to go for a shorter four week visit. Anna, though could not be persuaded "just in case Audrey gets a call" - sure enough it happened when it was least expected!

Anna and Adrian now stood at the door of the Intensive Care Unit, a very clinical double door arrangement implemented to help reduce airborne infections. Rolling up their sleeves, they scrubbed their hands, wrist and forearms in a procedure that would be repeated for every visit, reminding Adrian of the sad days visiting baby Anna. Every precaution was taken to protect Audrey from exposure to infection; she was too precious to be lost because of carelessness. In any transplant, the donor organ is seen as a foreign object and the recipient's body immediately attempts to destroy it by rejecting it. This mechanism defends healthy people from the many infections and diseases to which all are exposed every day. Perhaps the greatest breakthrough in transplant surgery in the last 30 years has been the use of immunosuppressant drugs to dampen the immune system to allow the donor organ to co-exist in the recipient. Getting the correct level of immunosuppressants is a complex task and in the first few days after transplant the immune system is at a very high level of suppression. This would leave Audrey very exposed to even simple things like skin borne infections or the common cold.

As Anna and Adrian entered the unit, Audrey looked like a person who was alive only because of machinery. The ventilator had been reduced after the crisis of the night before, and now the Novolung was removing the carbon dioxide from Audrey's blood. Into her neck were different lines of medicines, peaking at eight different substances being administered. She lay covered with just a thin sheet to preserve her dignity, completely sedated so that no part of her body could move. To stand and speak to Audrey was an incredibly difficult thing. She was unable to communicate back in any way, so different from the exciting communicator she normally was. The nursing staff explained the procedures, and one of the surgeons introduced himself. He had been working all night in charge of the ICU team and had been having a really tough time with Audrey. He had called upon all the skills he could call muster, but Adrian knew he had been guided by a Higher Hand.

Only the same two visitors were permitted into the intensive care unit, so the rest of the family could not enter the room. It was frustrating being so close to Audrey but unable to reach out and touch her and show their love. So they retreated from the hospital and drove a few miles to the scenic coast at Tynemouth, to sit in the car dozing, trying to come to terms with the events of the last 24 hours, wondering what hope there would be for Audrey.

Back at the hospital, another strange thing was happening. Audrey's blood pressure had quickly risen and had caused a blockage in the Novolung. As her new transplanted lung was essentially battered and bruised, the Novolung had provided necessary rest; now the surgeons had to disconnect it to clear the blockage. The strain of ventilation and processing carbon dioxide would return to Audrey's diseased lung and her transplanted lung. It was time of great tension. As the machinery of the Novolung was removed, the vital measurements began to show that the carbon dioxide levels were remaining steady, not rising as expected. Instead of the suffocating effects due to increasing carbon dioxide, she was actually managing well without the artificial lung. Something was happening beyond the physicians' control, but surely within the control of the Great Physician.

The diligence and care of the medical staff towards Audrey went far beyond the call of duty. Over her eyes they gently placed moisturising pads to help moisten them. The sedation had caused her to be fully asleep with her eyes open with no control over her eyelids. The sparkle of her eyes which had often defined her throughout her many tribulations was gone and Adrian longed for the lustre to return – he hoped it would be soon. He didn't know how to communicate to Audrey, so he began something that would become a signature of every visit - he began to sing! The nurses paused and listened to Adrian singing in the ICU. "Why not?" they thought. His signature song was the beautiful hymn by Philip Bliss,

Sing them over again to me, wonderful words of life,
Let me more of their beauty see, wonderful words of life;
Words of life and beauty teach me faith and duty.

Beautiful words, wonderful words, wonderful words of life,
Beautiful words, wonderful words, wonderful words of life.

As another evening passed and some sleep came, Audrey was having a comfortable night. Her blood pressure drugs were greatly reduced and her oxygen saturation was now at a very respectable level. One of the reasons for the good absorption of oxygen was the use of nitric oxide to help dilate the blood vessels and hence absorb more oxygen. This gas was another weapon in the extensive armoury in the hospital. As morning broke Audrey's ventilation had to be increased and her oxygen saturation had fallen. Adrian was plunged back into concern. He knew it would be a roller coaster ride, but he could not face it without the elation of a happy ending. The medical staff re-assured him that this situation was not unusual - her levels would oscillate and it was the long term, rather than the instantaneous readings that were important. These words of assurance gave some comfort, but Adrian was still obsessed over every figure on display.

The fragility of life yet again flashed before Adrian as he went out for a short walk with Anna and his brother Peter. Outside Freeman's hospital is a busy road, with a pedestrian crossing. They pressed the button to stop the traffic and started to cross the road, but just then a speeding taxi driver tried to jump the lights. Only Peter's observations and lightning fast reactions saved Anna from an almost certain death. The accelerating taxi driver regained control and then just laughed at the situation he had caused. Adrian, who is normally placid, could control his temper no longer, "Learn to drive!" he shouted and proceeded to note down the license details of the dangerous driver. "It must have been my adrenalin!" he later reflected.

Many men would not immediately choose their mother in law for their constant companion through the most stressful days of their life. But Adrian had no choice, he was stuck with Anna and she was stuck with him! It was to prove to be a very harmonious relationship. After all she was very similar in nature to Audrey. It was only Anna and Adrian who could see Audrey and they would have to work together to ensure the very best outcome for her. They agreed to try and keep their spirits high, no matter what the circumstances. They would find that they didn't need to look far to find something to laugh about. One evening they entered the waiting room outside intensive care to find another gentleman was using the room. It was still very warm in Newcastle, and the hospital heating was on full. It certainly wasn't a time for winter clothes. But this gentleman had taken health and safety just too seriously as he sat there with his winter jacket on and a building site safety helmet on his head. Adrian thought all this was strange, but more confusing the fact that he didn't appear to be visiting anyone in intensive care. He enjoyed his seat then headed home on the bus again, very safe from falling slates, metalwork or asteroids!

Adrian was trying to maintain normal life as much as possible, and he sat down to write a sympathy card to a recently bereaved widow. He wrote a scripture verse and sent it off to Perth. Almost as soon as the card went into the post box, Adrian realised that what he had written as scripture wasn't even in the Bible. "It sounded good to me," he laughed, "hope it helps!"

Audrey was making some visible signs of improvement. They had reduced her sedation and she now had her eyes open for a brief time. As Adrian spoke she was listening and when he kissed her, she tried to kiss him back. She also tried moving her left arm, a little glimmer of the real Audrey was shining through. Very quickly, though, she was back asleep as the medication took over.

The initial news on the 22nd of August was far less encouraging. Struggling to sleep, Adrian had been recalling the scripture, "In all thy ways acknowledge Him and He shall direct thy paths." The question could not leave him, "What does it mean to acknowledge Him?" He would find in experiences of acknowledging God he would even learn more of His perfect ways. Adrian rose just after 6am and called the hospital. The medical team had been struggling overnight, specifically they could not get Audrey's blood pressure under control. As the day moved on they were much happier and managed to reduce her adrenalin and her sedation. But as soon as they had tried to wash her she began to get distressed and they had to increase her sedation. Something was wrong that would take a few days to reveal itself. Overall the consultant was pleased with the slow but steady progress, and they were discussing the possibility of weaning her off the nitric oxide and waking her up. Adrian was hoping for the day when she would be fully awake once again. The next day, as the nurses were trying to move her to a different position on the bed, she again showed stress and needed increased ventilation and took a long time to recover. Adrian was disappointed that so little progress was being made. But at least he was pleased that she was now off the nitric oxide and now had only 5 lines in her neck. The latest addition was kidney dialysis to try and remove toxins in her body. She had begun to look puffy, part of the side effects of these toxins building up.

The problems of moving Audrey continued, and to compound matters, she was starting to get a bit red when lying on her right hand side. The most expensive and sophisticated mattresses couldn't avoid the distress of bed sores. Moving her to lie on her left side, the side of the transplanted lung, was impossible as her lung function fell too low and her heart beat rose rapidly. Progress was now very slow, in fact her artificial ventilation had been increased again and her temperature was now very low. They brought out the "Bear Hugger", a heated blanket system to try and keep her core temperature stable. Every possible effort was being made to ensure the greatest possibility of survival. By now the nurses were almost fighting to look after Audrey, a fascinating patient with a fighting spirit, and a prayer circle around the world.

With a gradual reduction in the sedation drugs, her eyes were starting to follow shapes and figures. To Adrian it was like a new born baby, following a moving finger or a light on the ceiling. She was also trying to speak, but ventilation going down her throat prevented this. As she tried to raise her arm, Adrian thought she sought a cuddle, but with her strength gone, her arm flopped at her side again. Now clearer in thought and mind Adrian turned to his little Bible to read to her. He remembered that hearing is one of the senses to continue even when others fail, so he read the lovely words of Mark chapter 6. But Audrey was agitated, her heart beat was increasing and she was becoming more restless. The doctors took Adrian and Anna aside to share their concerns: "We don't know if the left lung is doing anything." Adrian was stunned. The waiting had been hard, the transplant heart breaking, and now the possibility it was all in vain! Only time would tell if she would improve.

With Audrey, Anna and Adrian now staying in Newcastle, the Christians in the Tyneside area began to rally around, treating them just like one of their own. Homes were opened, meals were prepared, coffee stops were arranged, beds were made for visiting family, and earnest prayer was made. Rutherford Rabey of Wylam summarised it: "I have never seen such unity among the Christians, as at this moment." While Audrey lay in a critical condition in intensive care, no prayer time in Tyneside commenced without Audrey being first in the list for prayer. Her crises drove the Christians to their knees.

It was now the sixth day since the transplant and they had succeeded in getting Audrey to lie on her left side. Rejoicing at this little achievement, Anna and Adrian were hoping that perhaps the transplanted left lung was now starting to adjust to her body. Her sedation was the lowest so far, and amazingly she was now trying to express herself by blinking her eyes. The system was simple, Audrey blinks when she wants to give the answer to a question. When asked if she was in pain she gave a very fast and very deep blink - she was obviously feeling the pain of the treatment. Adrian plucked up courage to ask another question, "Do you want me to continue to sing?" He waited but her eyes failed to move. He wondered if this was a silent refusal. But he just couldn't stop, so he burst into song:

Safe am I, safe am I,
In the hollow of His hand;
Sheltered o'er, sheltered o'er
With His love forevermore
No ill can harm me, no foe alarm me,
For He keeps both day and night,
Safe am I, safe am I,
In the hollow of His hand.

Adrian sang this as a comfort to Audrey, and a tribute to the late Arthur Pollard who had ever engrained it in their minds. With the sedation reducing, Audrey was able to express facially a bit more of how she was feeling. Over her normally placid face was a look of fear and confusion. What was happening to her at that time was trapped inside her mind; only later would she be able to express something of the terrors she was going through due to very vivid hallucinations.

The 26th of August became another day of anguish for Audrey. The function of the left lung was still unclear, but the doctors had finally been able to diagnose the underlying problem. Adrian and Anna waited for the news. "We have found two issues," the doctor said, "some sort of blood clot in her lung and something else on the outside of her lung." They would be able to remove the clot inside her lung, but the clot on the outside would require further surgery. To enable surgery, an immediate reduction in anti-clotting drugs would have to commence, carrying its own risk, especially after the discovery of a clot inside the lung. The doctor had another therapy. "We'll turn the ventilation back up, and with the inside clot removed, we may be able to massage the lung into action." Adrian had to leave it to the experts and turned to provide Audrey with comfort from the scriptures. He read words from the Proverbs that he loved to use about her:

"Who can find a virtuous woman? For her price is far above rubies. The heart of her husband doth safely trust in her...She will do him good and not evil all the days of her life... Strength and honour are her clothing; and she shall rejoice in time to come...She openeth her mouth with wisdom; and in her tongue is the law of kindness. Many daughters have done virtuously, but thou excellest them all...Favour is deceitful, and beauty is vain: but a woman that feareth the LORD, she shall be praised."

By 6pm Audrey was taken back to theatre to remove the blood deposits on the outside of her lung. The experts hoped they had finally identified why she had made so little progress with her breathing. Adrian joked about getting a season pass for theatre - Audrey had become a regular visitor. But despite the outward frivolity, he felt flat again, another day on the roller coaster. Anna, Adrian, Adrian's mother Jean, and Audrey's sister Hazel all waited for further news. They shared the paper, completed the puzzles, paused for prayer and reflection, and generally checked their watches at regular intervals. Audrey's last visit to the theatre was expected to have a tragic outcome; they wondered what the result would be this time. It was not until 11pm when they received the news that surgery had been successful. A large collection of blood from beside her left lung had been removed and now they had been able to inflate her transplanted lung. This was the first really good news the family group had heard in days, and the surgeons were genuinely pleased. The nurse ended the conversation with, "They are exactly where we want them to be at the moment." As the group walked from the little flat they used at the hospital to the car, Adrian began to shake. The tension of the days had been very great, he was a bundle of nerves, and the cold night air cut him to the core. It had been a terrible trial so far.

When they returned to their residence, Adrian switched on the computer to find a further 54 e-mails in just the few hours they had waited for the surgery results. All over the world people were praying and following the story of Audrey's struggle. Adrian started the unwieldy task of replying to everyone, but it became an impossible burden. "I'll just publish all the details on an internet diary," he thought. Soon people were waiting eagerly for updates on their computers. Some would discuss what time Adrian would rise, or why was he so late at updates today? Some even wondered whose house they would be visiting, or what song he was singing today. In Perth a terminally ill friend of Audrey got herself a Bible and started to read the verses that Adrian had shared with Audrey. Adrian sighed, "Perhaps she will believe in Audrey's Saviour."

This further surgery became the turning point in Audrey's recovery. The early morning update had recorded that she had a very good night, her oxygen saturation improving, her ventilation reduced and her pain under control. The nurse cheerfully stated, "Going back to theatre has done Audrey the world of good." Adrian recalled the advice that he and Audrey were given as teenagers in Bible Class and he was sure this now completely contradicted it!

Anna and Adrian could barely wait for the visiting hour in the afternoon. He approached the nursing sister: "Audrey's sister has come all the way from Inverness - can she please see Audrey?" The strict 'two visitors only' policy was waived for the briefest of visits as Hazel approached Audrey and said, "Hi Audrey". Immediately Audrey opened her eyes, delighted to see her. Audrey again used her blinks to communicate - she is still in pain, she liked Adrian's new shirt and jumper, and now she even enjoys his singing. The nurse suggested that they could bring in a CD player and let her listen to CDs. Things were starting to look up, Audrey was even cosy again. The CD of Amy Grant went on, and simply looped around days on end. Whenever it stopped she signalled for it to play again. She was resting on the sentiments, "Rock of Ages cleft for me, let me hide myself in Thee."

With this progress, the most simple physiotherapy could begin. It started with wiggling her toes, opening her mouth and holding the nurse's hand - impossible exercises a few days earlier. As she began to take these steps forward, Adrian and Anna were busy hosting even more visitors. Many friends of Audrey's were determined to get to Newcastle, even though she herself could not receive visitors. It seemed to bring them emotionally closer to Audrey. Bitten Campbell became the gracious hostess, with Audrey's friends and family being able to make themselves at home! With Audrey less sedated, the ventilation through a tube into her mouth became a bigger issue - it was making her sick and she was attempting to bite through the tubing. So the medical team prepared to give Audrey a tracheotomy - her fourth surgical procedure within ten days. This would allow her to be fully awake, possibly able to cough, but unable to speak in the short term. But she looked scared as she awaited further surgery. Using head nods, she pleaded with Adrian to stay, but he had to leave the professionals to complete another delicate procedure.

Adrian paced around waiting for the procedure to be completed, wondering why it was taking so long. In the intensive care unit, she was not only getting a tracheotomy but they had to put her back onto dialysis as her kidneys had stopped working. She was also being faced with some kind of stomach bypass to prevent her being sick. Anna had been very strong in the midst of all the trial, although alone, with John still thousands of miles away in Singapore. John himself was struggling to concentrate, worried yet so helpless, and feeling so distant from everything. Mercifully his hosts were doctors who were able to explain the intricacies of the medical procedures.

Next morning would begin Audrey's first day fully awake. Adrian pondered the prospect of seeing her awake again, and began to wonder what these missing ten days would have felt like to her. Before she could receive visitors, the nurses washed her hair, cut her nails and ensured she would look her best. As 3pm came, Adrian entered the ICU and she was fully awake - it was a wonderful sight. She was still heavily medicated, but much of her sparkle had returned and she even wanted to start writing again. But with her strength so diminished, she couldn't hold a pen - it would improve with time. After just a short visit, her demeanour changed and she seemed sleepy and quite indifferent.

Adrian began again to speak to her, "Darling, you have had a lung transplant." Audrey gave him the most vivid of looks and expressed without words, "Have I?" It was a total surprise to her. He then told her about all the other procedures, and again she seemed oblivious to them all. She was shocked by all this news. This became a regular topic of conversation as her drugs made her drowsy and unable to remember exactly what had been said. At least for Adrian it was fun to be able to see her expression of surprise each time! But he must have been a little dopey as he started to sing a medley of songs, but could remember only the first lines. But there seemed little that he could do to try and cheer her up. She wouldn't sleep and she had a constant look of agitation, looking so very sad and unhappy. Audrey very rarely got downhearted. "It must be all the medication that is affecting her," he concluded. Then he thought of another reason, "How would I feel if I got fed vanilla milkshakes down my nose day after day?" he laughed. "Surely Audrey won't want a milkshake for years to come!"

In the morning Adrian turned and looked at the calendar. It was the last day in August, and for a whole month Audrey and Adrian had been away from home - first their holidays, and then the transplant. Adrian wondered why he didn't miss home more, and then he concluded, "Home is where Audrey is." Home for them was Newcastle just now. At least medically she was really starting to make some progress, with the cumbersome ventilator replaced with a gentler almost domestic type of ventilator. Adrian was determined to try and bring her as much cheer as possible. "Perhaps I could get Ian Campbell in to visit Audrey," he said to Anna. "How can you manage that?" she said. "We'll call it a pastoral visit!" Ian was delighted to be her pastor that afternoon and he read Isaiah 43 and prayed with her. She enjoyed the visit but kept looking at the clock rather impatiently. It was only later that she was able to explain that she had been suffering from many lucid hallucinations during these trying days. As Ian was sitting with her, Audrey thought the hospital was being broken into and Ian's car vandalised. She wondered how he was so calm!

Anna and Adrian would have another change ahead of them that evening. While in Newcastle, Ian and Bitten had sacrificed their home, beds, food and time for them. Anna and Adrian didn't want to abuse this kindness, and just then another friend Marian Rixham gave them the keys to her house and said, "I'm away for two weeks, have my house and stay as long as you like." They were being showered with kindness. They would rest well that evening, looking forward to seeing if Audrey would be up out of bed tomorrow.

As the new month commenced, so a new day dawned in Audrey's recovery. True to the experts' word, she was up sitting in a chair. The nurses had been so kind, a small army of staff moved her using a hoist and her radiant face told of her joy at being able to sit up again. It was obvious though that the surgery had been hard on her; she was thin, with limp muscles and little strength to hold herself up in the chair. Her greatest treat was to receive into her mouth tiny sponges filled with water. Nothing had passed her lips for many days - she drank every drop. As Adrian turned to the scriptures to read, she was now more able to follow the lovely words of John 17 and 18.

Later that day, the physiotherapist arrived to initiate an exercise programme. They have often been called the 'physio-terrorists' - to some people their programmes seemed like torture! Audrey had been told that post-transplant they would make her work hard. Thankfully their treatment of Audrey was very gentle as she could hold only the smallest of weights.

As the days began to roll by more quickly, Audrey's nurses became more adventurous with her. One gave her tea on a sponge instead of water. Another gave her the tiniest piece of chocolate, to Audrey it tasted heavenly. Adrian was sent out to purchase what the Geordies call "Ice Pops", frozen flavoured water to be given her at the appropriate moment. Now she was enquiring what Anna and Adrian had themselves been eating, her mind now dreaming about food that tasted better than vanilla milkshakes.

With a measure of strength returning, she was determined to start writing again. She picked up a pen and paper and after several minutes of writing, Adrian looked down - it was completely illegible! He didn't know quite what to say, so he asked, "Have they given you a Chinese lung?" She was at least able to see the funny side of her frustration. Things were also changing for Adrian, as he would have to start working again, part time, in a new office with colleagues he had never met before. For Anna, it was good news that John had managed to get back safely from Singapore and would soon be joining them in Newcastle. Life was starting to look more promising. The next stage was to reduce Audrey's ventilation further and if possible get her onto her feet for a few minutes.

Audrey's strength had returned enough to hold the pen to write something legible. Adrian wondered what her first words would be. He waited for her writing to stop. Her first words were, "What about camp?" He replied, "Why are you thinking about camp, it's all under control?" With all the hours she had for thinking, her mind was starting to return to normal life and responsibility. The previous year's camp had been the first one she had not been well enough to attend for the whole week, and she longed for a return to health so she could get fully involved again. She had nothing to worry about - in the midst of her crisis, others had risen to the challenge and the camp was going forward.

Now that she could write a few words again, her next challenge was to be able to speak. This would be a difficult one, as a tracheotomy hinders normal vibrations in vocal cords. But another great invention was at hand to help her. David Muir, an American quadriplegic suffering with muscular dystrophy, had a severe respiratory arrest in 1984. He was rushed to hospital and had a tracheotomy was inserted. He was devastated, now unable to speak or move. While recovering he studied the equipment and invented a valve which would allow him to speak, and also breathe. Together with a Dr Passy, they perfected the Passy-Muir valve. This simple but ingenious invention has enabled many tracheotomy users to speak.

The nurse carefully inserted the Passy-Muir valve and within seconds Audrey was speaking again. It was more squeaking then speaking, but another little sparkle of hers returned again. Audrey spoke a lot, "It's great to be able to communicate!" The questions then poured out, "What had happened during surgery, who had performed it, why hadn't it gone so well, what has been happening since then?" So many questions, not all of them easily answered in the few minutes at the hospital bed. For Adrian some of the questions were easy to answer, "Who's looking after Tinkerbell?" Tinkerbell the cat was getting well looked after by Audrey's sister Moira, so Audrey would be able to rest better that night with some of her questions answered.

Progress was becoming more marked every day. Audrey was now able to stand, with assistance, for four minutes a day. The nurses had managed to get her into a normal hospital chair, and she could now sit like a queen and receive her guests. Her sense of humour was also starting to return as she started to write the essence of a joke: "How do you eat an elephant? In small pieces!" Yet this was how she had faced this seemingly insurmountable trial. So Adrian dashed out and purchased a toy elephant as a reminder of her returning health and humour. Despite the progress made, however, she was still tired and needed a further blood transfusion - she was certainly not out of the woods yet.

Every day dozens of cards arrived at the hospital for her. One of the nurses stopped Adrian and asked, "Is Audrey some sort of celebrity?" Adrian laughed, "She is kind of famous now!" She treasured every card and has kept them all in safe storage ever since.

Audrey was still very fragile, tired, and was now shaky, one of the side effects of the anti-rejection medicine. As Adrian sat down to read the Bible, Audrey began to write, "I need the peace of God." Still anxious and upset, after enduring an ongoing trauma it was understandable that she would be emotional. But she had found relief in writing and was now constantly scribbling on her notepad, even making plans for Adrian to tidy up around her bed to ensure everything was in its correct place. But now a further dilemma - she couldn't differentiate between myth and reality due to the hallucinations' – another task for Adrian to sort out. She wrote to him, "You and mum are my only link with reality; I really appreciate your visits." In a further test she had to drink a dye which was then checked to ensure it had not entered her lungs. "Can I get to drink from a cup?" she asked - a major breakthrough that she longed for.

Back in Perth the Sunday School was about to start again. This would be the first year Audrey had not been involved in it since she had been a small girl. She longed to be with the leaders, but it looked increasingly likely that Newcastle might be her home until Christmas. But now she had other delights to experience - her very own cup of tea. She had passed the fluids test and was now determined to drink as much as possible to help her kidneys start working again. The daily dialysis at 4am was exhausting and she longed to be free from this artificial aid as well as from the ventilation now being reduced. She was finally permitted to see her Dad after his trip to Singapore and his quarantine at Freeman's. It was such a relief for father and daughter to be reunited. She had found a comfortable position in bed, she sat with her music playing, with her pink "lollipops" and she exclaimed, "This is truly heavenly!" (Adrian wondered if perhaps this definition was a little over generous!) Her pink lollies were quickly forgotten when the next delight came on - strawberry yoghurt (even though it was blue!). This helped her gain a little strength so that she could be helped to stand - and to make a few steps in a circle. She was even managing to speak very quietly without her speaking valve. It was amazing the progress she was making.

John, Anna and Adrian set off for another visit to the hospital. In her rush Anna had left a solitary curler in her hair. John didn't notice, and Adrian didn't want to say to his mother in law, but

Audrey now gaining strength and awareness quickly pointed it out. The intensive care department was filled with laughter as that curler was removed and hidden in the handbag. Audrey was now on real food with Weetabix for breakfast, soup and semolina for lunch and drinks during the day. She was now able to sit in a chair from 8am until 4pm, and she enjoyed Adrian reading Philippians chapter 4, especially as she so longed for peace. The specialists had also managed to reduce her ventilation to only 1 hour of high pressure ventilation in a 20 hour period. Audrey was struggling to see her progress but it was happening rapidly in front of everyone's eyes. God was answering the thousands of prayers made daily for her. The next day, she had moved on from semolina to "real food", to roast lamb; it was wonderful after weeks being fed through the nose.

The 13th of September became a red letter day in Audrey's life. The day before they had been testing her with only oxygen into the tracheotomy site and no ventilation. She had managed 24 hours on this so her consultants now decided that she was well enough to leave intensive care and to go on to the next stage of rehabilitation, the high supervision ward where she would have her own bedroom and one nurse shared among four patients. She had received the highest of medical care and had spent an amazing and humbling 25 days learning what the will of God meant to her. They were all so deeply grateful for the all care she had received.

CHAPTER 13

Recovery

On the 13th of September 2008, Audrey entered the relative freedom of Ward 27a. This was a very small facility with only five rooms. These were usually occupied by either those critically ill and waiting for a transplant or those making progress after their transplant. She was delighted to be in this very special place where she could receive her visitors at any reasonable time. There was even a small kitchen where they could make a cup of tea.

The most valued immediate change was that her room had a window. The tiny windows of ICU were behind her bed so she had lain for 25 days and nights with no views of the sky. Now daylight and a view of the courtyard below where she could watch children, recovering from heart surgery, bounding with energy.

The nurses had every intention of pushing Audrey hard in her recovery but she still felt so very fragile. Her body was weak, her breathing was recovering only slowly, she could barely stand and she felt emotionally drained. She had not even starting taking her medication herself. It seemed like an impossible road.

They sat down to reflect on what had been happening. They wondered about sending a message to their family. Adrian thought for a moment, "Why don't we make a video to send to them?" he said. So a camera was set up ready to record a few comments from Audrey. As she stared at the camera, she panicked, "What am I going to say?" Since transplant she had barely needed to make one decision, she was still not clear thinking and her confidence was low. Adrian steadied her nerves and gave her the basis of a little talk to camera. Like a true professional, she only needed one take as word perfect she addressed the camera. They then sat down to copy the videos and send them to the family - they were back in action working together as a team!

Audrey's family presented her with a lovely gift to treasure. From a shop where toy bears were made to your own specification they chose one with a voice recorder inside it. They huddled around the recording machine and gave their own personal greeting to Audrey. When she pressed the body of the bear, it gave her family's message of love. Touched by their thoughtfulness she has given this bear a special place ever since.

In the evening, the dreaded moment came when Audrey had to organise her own medication to take orally. The anti-rejection drugs were sized like giant bullets! She nearly cried when she saw the size of these capsules. "I'll never manage these no matter how much water I drink," she said. The nurse saw her predicament, "Try it with milk!" So placing it in her mouth and swallowing with her milk, capsule number one reached its target. This was only the beginning - there were tablets to be taken every few hours, dozens every day. Each of them had a vital function, some even were to deal with the side effects of other ones! Perhaps the most amazing medicine was the immunosuppressant drugs, designed to prevent the lung being rejected by her body. As early as 1957, employees of the Sandoz company were asked to bring back to work soil samples from the places they visited on holiday. Samples came from all over the world, but most failed to lead to any valuable breakthroughs in pharmacology. One of them, though, brought back from Hardangervidda National Park in Norway, showed amazing characteristics which had not been seen before. This was to provide a breakthrough in transplant medicine, leading to the development of the drug Cyclosporin.

Once the ordeal of the medicine taking was over, Audrey was

ready to get some much needed sleep. As Adrian started to pack up his few belongings and head back to his residence, she had one further comment, "Where did you get those clothes?" The £10 clothes from ASDA had been well worn but now sadly failed to meet her approval. It was a sign that some of her sparkle was returning. So it again became Audrey's advice for the next choice of wardrobe!

Next morning, when Adrian phoned Audrey he was put straight through to her room. It was like a hotel, with her own receptionist and even room service! She had an exciting proposition, "Come for lunch today; they will allow you to purchase it in the restaurant and you can bring it back here." Adrian felt like a teenager again on a date with his lovely girlfriend. It had been a long time since she had invited him to lunch; he was looking forward to the treat. She was also preparing for the next step back to reality, "Bring the laptop, so I can read the e-mails." Adrian agreed, but he wondered if she realised quite how many e-mails there would be to read!

The change from intensive care to greater independence had a profound and rapid effect on Audrey's improvement. She was able to have a shower, a pleasant change from the indignity of a bed bath. Her breathing was improving, with a greatly reduced need for oxygen. Her only pipe work was now her tracheotomy, which she was sure would soon be removed. Things were looking up. Just at this bright moment the fire alarm sounded in the ward. The nurses were planning the patient evacuation - their worst nightmare, evacuating five critically ill patients, all the machinery and doing so safely. Just before the evacuation commenced, the Fire and Rescue Service arrived. They found the crisis was only a little cooking accident! A patient's visitor had placed his meal in a microwave and selected 60 minutes instead of 60 seconds. After 60 minutes the food was so well cooked it was on fire. The smell of melted plastic and burnt cooking lasted for days. Soon visitors were strictly banned from anything more complicated than boiling a kettle!

The excitement of the 'inferno' was a further catalyst for Audrey to get back on her feet. She wanted to be able to make a run for it, in case of another blaze! The physiotherapists arrived, "Audrey, let's go for a walk." She hesitated, she hadn't walked properly in weeks. Could she manage? Slowly but surely, she moved her feet forward. This was no race of speed but one that required patience and endurance. She set her eyes on the goal, "I'll reach the end of the ward!" and then she was off. With the adulation for this Olympic feat completed, she retreated to bed for some further rest.

Then the next challenge arrived - it was time to leave the near sterile environment of the ward and meet a limited selection of other people. "Audrey, please can you go down for an X-ray," instructed the nurse. Adrian was delighted; he was back to pushing her wheelchair, racing along the quiet corridors. This was their first trip out together since the transplant and they savoured every minute at the romantic X-ray department! As they returned from X-ray, another surprise was awaiting them - it was time to remove the tracheotomy. Soon, holding down the sticker placed over the hole in her trachea, she was able to talk freely again. It was time to celebrate with the luxury of hospital fish and chips.

It was now four weeks since the night of the transplant and the transformation in Audrey was truly amazing. She slept well, satisfied that progress was being made and rejoicing in God's goodness. The Fergusons reflected on what God had done, it was nothing short of miraculous. God was certainly still on His throne. When she rose next morning, the physiotherapists were set for the day ahead, "Okay Audrey, today you are going to the gym." She looked reluctant. "The gym, I've only got my pyjamas!" They laughed, "You'll look great!" Off they set for another exciting stage in her recovery, with little or no strength, but obediently wanting to complete the set exercise plan.

But her tiredness did not lift, and the next day her breathing statistics were worse. The specialists arrived and with serious faces pondered her condition. Here was another challenge medically. It could be one of three possibilities - tiredness, infection, or a rejection. The word 'rejection' struck fear into Adrian's heart. After all she had passed through, he was shocked that rejection could still bring a bleak prognosis. The consultant carefully explained, "Nearly every transplant patient suffers rejections. These are most common in the first six months. It is part of the process of getting the anti-rejection drugs at the correct level." Now a very high dosage of steroids would be given to virtually eradicate her immune system, leaving her very susceptible to infection and she would need to be isolated for at least three days. By 9:30pm she was exhausted, desperately needing some sleep.

In the morning, her condition had deteriorated even further. She had slept poorly, there had been much to think about, especially the potential rejection. She turned to look at her legs, now sore and swollen. Fluid was building up in them, almost in front of her eyes, adding a further 10 kgs to her already exhausted frame. The physiotherapists arrived, but it was no day for exercise. She attempted some movements, but could barely muster the energy to converse with her many carers. Adrian felt low. Strangely, despite her weakness Audrey's spirits were buoyed up. Her friend Alison had sent her a special edition of the Radio Bible Class, "Our Daily Bread". As she started to read it the pages of precious scripture and comments lifted her to another sphere. This little book would become her constant companion, like manna from heaven.

A friendly nurse entered the room, "I thought I could tell you a little about treatment for rejection." Her gentle tone was reassuring, "You'll probably be up doing cartwheels after the steroids!" Audrey hadn't done cartwheels for a few years, but she was willing to give them another try. But with the fluid on her legs now reaching her lower back it was becoming increasingly painful, and cartwheels seemed a distant possibility.

On the 19th of September, she started the steroid treatment. The drip was set up and the needle into her vein, so that for the next hour steroids would infuse into her blood and her immune system would be lowered. The dosage would be 50 times higher than a normal maintenance dose. They joked, "enough for a horse!" She was now back into isolation with only Anna and Adrian as her companions. Instead of it being dreary and sad, she felt a bit better and by the evening she was so much brighter. She even did some weight lifting in her bed! In isolation, she became a great encouragement to Anna and Adrian, speaking of how she had felt like Job in scripture and the despair he had experienced. Despite her trials she was conscious of God's help right beside her. Adrian wrote about his worries: "We know it doesn't help, we know it can show a lack of faith, but we still seem to do it. I suppose we tend to worry about the things that might happen tomorrow, yet God never promises anyone tomorrow, He simply gives us one day at a time. The future does look unclear and the journey seems hard, but I recall the words I quoted at my wedding in 1994, 'I do not know what lies ahead, the way I cannot see; yet one stands there to be my friend, He'll show the way to me'."

Day 2 on her rejection treatment, was not the dramatic improvement Audrey had hoped for, she actually felt worse. Adding to the fluid on her legs was the general puffiness that steroids give and she now felt very uncomfortable. Again she was struggling with peace, so Adrian turned again to Philippians 4, exactly the verses required for that day. At this low point an amazing present arrived all the way from New Zealand. A family Audrey only knew through e-mail sent the most beautiful box of gifts, including ingredients for baking when she got home, songs to sing, music to play, a DVD to watch and even a flag to wave. The highlight was the individual letters from the mother, father and their six children. God had exercised Gordon and Coralie McLay's hearts to send cheer, exactly when it was required.

The final day on the high dosage steroids, saw her feeling a fraction better again. It was not quite the rapid progress the hospital had hoped for but it certainly was progress. Her oxygen stats had marginally improved, her X-ray and her badly swollen legs were also showing some improvements. This was just the catalyst to get her back to her exercise programme, on her exercise pedals and lifting weights again. "Perhaps tomorrow, I'll be back at the gym," she stated optimistically. She continued to receive five star treatment, with nurses running to meet her every need and even bacon and eggs for breakfast! Bowing her head she thanked God for the excellent care she was receiving.

But there was yet another unwelcomed shock in the morning. A nurse approached Audrey's room, visibly upset. She said, "Audrey I have bad news, your room is desperately needed for another patient; we'll have to relocate you to another ward." Audrey was shocked, she had only been in Ward 27a for a few days, in three of which she was isolated due to rejection. She began to weep, "How can this be? I'm not well enough to leave the unit." The decision, though, had been made; she would not be able to change it. As she tried to come to terms with this change, she read the news that Freeman's hoped to build Europe's largest transplant centre. This was too late for her but she was pleased that other patients would be able to benefit. Even the move to the new room did not go smoothly and by the end of the afternoon she was feeling upset and emotional. At the consultant's visit, there was better news - she was improving, but it was going to take a long time. They satisfied themselves that they would be spending Christmas in Newcastle. Their scripture reading that evening was in Psalm 22, and Adrian noted, "Psalm 22 is amazing. We saw it in a different light today - the feeling of helplessness, but also the help that comes from the Lord. Audrey very much feels lacking in human strength but she draws her help from the Lord."

The next day brought a lovely contrast from the gloom of previous day. Music was ringing through the corridors of Freeman's Hospital! Audrey and Adrian went along for a visit to the hospital chapel - a true oasis of peace in the midst of trauma and trouble. In the chapel was a beautiful piano. Adrian moved the wheelchair to the edge of the piano and Audrey began to play some sweet music. She couldn't remember all the notes, her mind was still unclear, but she could remember enough to make a beautiful melody. The chapel became a frequent haven of rest for Audrey and her many visitors. Within a day, she was starting to feel stronger again and she was back at the gym pushing herself to her limits. Her scars were starting to heal and her spirits were brighter. She even managed to connect into her bank account to examine how well Adrian had managed their finances in her absence.

As September drew to a close, Audrey was making large strides forward every day. Her swollen legs were starting to reduce and her feet were again strong enough to stand on. She could even walk unaided along the hospital corridor, without it having any effect on her breathing statistics. Another friend, Rutherford Rabey became a regular visitor. They retreated to the chapel for another special time where she played the piano and Rutherford read the scriptures. She even managed to smuggle an ice cream and her favourite crisps into the chapel - probably a bit unorthodox but she concluded, "It was very tasty." Days seemed to become busier with longer walks, teaching sessions from the nurses on 'life after transplant', and the ongoing cycle of adjusting to medication. Her last visible prop, her oxygen, was finally removed. This was a major milestone as she had been on oxygen for about 15 hours a day for several years, a familiar sight around Perth, pushing her oxygen trolley or with her liquid oxygen "jet pack". She felt this would be like someone recovering from a leg break and having to throw away the crutches. She thought, "Can I manage?" She managed, in fact as the days rolled on, she never noticed it wasn't there. She was visibly improving.

It started only as a whisper among the nurses but soon the secret was out: "We want to send Audrey home, perhaps in a week's time." It was nowhere near Christmas, the earliest expected time of leaving the hospital. "Could this really be possible?" wondered Adrian, there seemed so much improvement yet to be made. There was no halfway house facility available, so the next step would have to be the massive one of returning home. Audrey's whole family agreed, "We will help her get the best care possible at home." They were prepared for the additional burden, but also the great privilege of caring for her.

But before home could even be contemplated, she would need to be happy about leaving hospital safely. "Tomorrow, you can have a day trip out," said the senior nurse. "I recommend fish and chips from Tynemouth; you won't catch any bugs off them!" Adrian was given detailed instructions - he was to meet Audrey at 11am and then take her out. As he arrived, she was all ready for the day trip. She walked along the corridor, down the lift and out to the front door. It took a long while, but she achieved it and Adrian suspected it wouldn't be too long before she was racing him along the hallways. The short drive along the coast was a wonderful tonic for her, able to breathe in fresh air and enjoy its effects on her new lung. After the delicious fish and chips, Ian and Bitten arrived to take her further along the coast. It was a happy day, her first taste of the outside world after the transplant. When she returned to Freeman's she was exhausted and so straight back to bed for a rest, satisfied that things were going in the right direction.

Over the next few days, Adrian and Audrey had fun reading through the hospital literature and spotting mistakes. As they read the Transplant Guide they noted: "All frozen food must be kept at below -150 degrees centigrade." This was much colder than the South Pole, and most domestic freezers can only reach -23 degrees centigrade! They then turned to the cooking section and spotted the recommendation: "All food should be cooked to 750 degrees centigrade." They wondered how they would ever reach these temperatures without burning their house down. Then a further mistake stood out: "Chilled food should be kept between 0 to 50 deg centigrade." It seemed that the person tasked with typing the manual had added an extra zero to every figure! Friends began to share their experiences of similar mistakes in print. A particularly funny one came from Roman Road Hall in Motherwell. The fire alert sign said, "In the event of a fire, evacuate the building, only when you are sure it is a false alarm." Audrey laughed, "What would they do if it was not a false alarm?"

The transplant had had another strange result. The more Audrey spoke the more people were puzzled. "Why does she sound so different?" The reason was that she still had a hole in her neck, which was healing only very slowly. This meant her vocal cords could get only limited vibrations. Her niece thought she had become a Glaswegian, and Audrey herself thought she had a Fife accent. Add to that her Chinese handwriting, she would be returning home a lot more cosmopolitan than before. She laughed - she would just be like the children from Junior Camp who return home with a new accent after a week with others from all over the country.

The last day in September arrived and Audrey looked at the calendar. It was her wedding anniversary. When Adrian arrived, he presented her with a new watch, a special gift for a special person. She looked at him, "I have a card for you but I haven't managed out to buy you anything!" He laughed, "I'm very disappointed you didn't make the effort. What have you been doing for the last few weeks?" The atmosphere was joyful; they could celebrate the anniversary that never looked like it would be possible. The doctors also had an interesting present for Audrey - a CD with pictures of all her X-rays. Not many people can boast about having a family album with X-ray images.

The quieter evening gave them time to chat and reflect on the experiences they had been passing through. Audrey said, "I don't expect life will ever be the same again. I don't want to be a celebrity, but I also don't want to slip back into the way we lived before the transplant." It would be a challenge to adjust after the agony and ecstasy of the months she had passed through. Audrey quoted her special verse, 'For I know the plans I have for you,' declares the Lord, 'plans to prosper you and not to harm you, plans to give you hope and a future.' (Jeremiah 29:11). It had been an anniversary they would never forget.

Flipping over the calendar, Audrey was shocked. She had arrived in August and now it was October. It was the longest time that she had ever been away for home. Adrian reflected, "It has been quite an amazing experience, we have learned loads about the Lord, ourselves and our family. We have learned much about what is important and what is not. I wonder if perhaps one day Audrey and I will write it all down in a book so that others can laugh and cry with us."

The doctor came with the message, "Tomorrow, I think it will be time for you to go home." Audrey was elated, "I'm going home, let's have a party." That evening, John, Anna, Audrey and Adrian sat and enjoyed orange juice and fairy cakes, their best party ever. Adrian stayed up late to write another entry in his internet diary which was being followed by thousands of people. He had a last contribution to make. "The next planned entry will hopefully say we are home safely, and after that I'm afraid it will be back to normal life and probably very few entries. Many thanks to all who have read these notes, e-mailed, visited, provided food, sent gifts and especially provided accommodation. The hymn writer said:

> How good is the God we adore,
> Our faithful unchangeable Friend,
> His love is as great as His power
> And knows neither measure nor end.

We fully agree and hope our experiences might be a help and encouragement for you to 'Look up'. P.S. watch the Asda Share Price fall."

On the 2nd of October 2008, Audrey left Freeman's Hospital and they headed home to Methven. It was a very safe and comfortable journey.

CHAPTER 14

Returning Home – Stars over Methven

When Audrey left Freeman's, she felt wrapped in cotton wool, her feet resting on a sleeping bag, her swollen legs and feet elevated. With her head and back resting on pillows, Adrian drove his princess carefully home in their carriage! As they entered Methven, there was the welcoming sight of their house festooned with balloons and banners: "Welcome Home – Audrey". It was like a gala day in Methven as a welcoming party of neighbours and family greeted Audrey. She had been sorely missed.

Now it was time for her to make her break for freedom. "I'll walk up the path myself, I won't need the wheelchair", she said. Slowly she stepped out of the car and steadied herself. With a fixed eye on the door, she walked past the banners and balloons straight into the house. Adrian recalled the romance of 1994 when he had carried Audrey over the threshold of their first home. She was determined that in 2008 she would not need carried, she would be very happy to walk.

Audrey felt ecstatic to be home again. There were no set visiting hours, no 'two visitors to a bed' rules, and no sleeping with the light on! Visitors flooded in, they had missed seeing Audrey and they were excited about catching up with her again. "We're only coming in for a minute," they said, but Audrey would reply, "Stay longer, I feel fine." The kettle was constantly on the boil and many eager helpers rallied round to serve tea and home baking. Tasty meals were delivered by family and friends from the Gospel Hall. Adrian and Audrey could sit down and enjoy eating proper meals together again.

As night fell, Audrey tried her best to get to sleep, but by 4am, they were sitting eating cookies and drinking tea. The excitement of being home and the effect of the steroids made sleep impossible. It would be months before she would enjoy a near normal sleep pattern again.

In the morning the door bell rang, her team of helpers were there to get her ready for the day. One of the more difficult issues was an open wound in her back. During the post-transplant investigation, the transplant entry was re-opened, but it was not possible to stitch it up again fully. The surgeon pulled back the dressing to show Adrian - he gulped, "It was like an axe wound." It would take over nine months to seal up, with a nurse coming diligently every few days to pour silver solution into the wound and dress it again. After her medical needs were dealt with, more visitors arrived to spend precious time with her - she was overwhelmed to be surrounded by such love.

By mid afternoon, she was ready for some rest, "I'm heading to bed for ten minutes, please don't go away, I won't be long." Ten minutes passed and Adrian went to check up on her. Her face looked puffy and when she spoke her voice sounded different. He was puzzled, but little seemed to surprise him any more. But as she rose to speak to her family, it was obvious that something was wrong. They joked, "We know who has been eating all the biscuits!" Her face had swollen up like a balloon and her speech resembled the sound of Mickey Mouse. It was possible to tap her face and hear crackles under the skin. They thought they'd better call the NHS emergency line. An ambulance with paramedics soon arrived. Within seconds they had drawn their conclusion, "It could be a spider bite!" Adrian was bemused at their logic. "She has just had lung transplant, could it not possibly be a problem linked to that?" Amid much confusion the ambulance team rushed her through to the large Ninewells Hospital in Dundee.

The now familiar routine of X-rays, breathing tests and

examinations started, and Audrey was disappointed to be in hospital within only a few days of her discharge. It was even more difficult as she was placed in the medical admissions ward on a busy Saturday evening - it was hectic with admissions from fights, drinking and self abuse. A selection of Dundee's busy nightlife was there in case she needed company! With so many people to attend to, the ward round was greatly delayed and it was 2am until she was examined. Holding up the X-ray, the doctor concluded: "It is not immediately life threatening tonight, so don't worry," and he swiftly moved on to the next patient. It was little comfort to Audrey to get no known reason for her predicament. On Sunday morning, she was transferred to somewhere more secluded, the Infectious Diseases Ward! - used to treat TB patients and those in the final stages of AIDS disease. It did little to raise her spirits, but it was the best place to keep away airborne infections. A highly skilled consultant was specially called in to see her. As he examined the X-ray, he could notice that oxygen had leaked from her old damaged (right) lung into her chest cavity and skin, a condition called "Surgical Emphysema". They were relieved that it was not something more serious. The symptoms, though, were hard for Audrey who was concerned that visitors would be shocked at her "Elephant Face". Thankfully as the evening progressed some of the symptoms reduced and she hoped it would disappear as fast as it had come.

As Adrian drove home, the road had been salted as the temperatures had plunged to 2 degrees centigrade. He laughed, "2 degrees is a pleasant change from constantly recording Audrey's core temperature of 37 degrees!" Reaching home, he gazed at the sky, and wrote down, "The stars were beautiful tonight over Methven." Later he recalled the words of scripture: "The heavens declare the glory of God; and the firmament sheweth His handywork." As he beheld the beauty, the awesome display of the greatness of his God, he gasped. Not one star was out of place, not one falling to the ground, all kept in place by the hand of God. How puny he felt standing before the great and mighty God who was revealing His creation to him. The phrase "stars over Methven" became precious to him as he considered this very personal revelation of God that evening.

The next day, Audrey got home. The consultants in Dundee had recommended that she return for a further examination in Newcastle. Adrian was glad he had never said anything bad about Newcastle in his internet diary! They rose at 5am and drove straight down. Freeman's gave Audrey a detailed CT scan to try to find where the air had come from. The results soon revealed that her old right lung had indeed attempted to collapse, but due to earlier treatment in Edinburgh it had failed. She was so relieved, worrying in case something sinister was wrong. Unfortunately there was one further procedure to do the next day, so she had another long night to pass in the hospital.

Next morning she was given a bronchoscopy, passing a video camera down her trachea into her lungs. The consultant brought some cheer, "Don't worry; I've had it done to myself four times without anaesthetic, just to demonstrate it!", "Why would anyone do this for demonstration purposes?" she wondered. "That is impressive commitment to medicine!" The bronchoscopy confirmed that there was indeed nothing more sinister and she would be able to return home after another night's observation. As she obeyed her final hospital curfew, Adrian was able to say goodbye to their special Newcastle friends. That night was the final sailing of the famous ship, the QE2, leaving Tyneside for retirement in Dubai. Adrian and his friends gathered at the quayside to watch her sail into the darkness. As they stood and watched there was a spectacular fireworks display. Adrian quipped, "It's amazing how they put these on for Audrey!" It might have been the end of an era for the QE2, but it was the beginning of a wonderful new era for Audrey.

Now that she was home again, recuperation could commence

in earnest. The Fergusons' neighbours gave them free use of their treadmill and Audrey measured her every footstep forward. Every night she recorded her temperatures, her breathing statistics, her blood pressure and her distance covered. She had experienced several set backs, now she only wanted to go forward. For Adrian it was time to return to his work, back to his normal job and his usual desk, for the first time in seven weeks. He was so grateful that his team had coped without him despite difficulties they encountered.

As life settled back into more of a normal routine for Audrey, she started to publish some of her comments to help others. One of the first things she wrote was,

"Well a lot has happened since I last spoke to you all and really I am just starting to be able to bring together the surreal life that I have been living with 'normal' life. As you probably all know … things didn't run quite as smoothly as they could have at the start, and well, I appear to have missed a few weeks of my life, but heh, what's a few weeks when you look back later in life!

"I would be lying if I said it has all been a pleasant experience, but I would say it has been one which has brought me closer to the Lord and made me cling on as this clearly was the only important thing to do - nothing else mattered. It's amazing how we think our life is important, the mundane things I mean, but when it comes down to it, it can all be done by others, probably more ably, and the only thing that matters is our relationship with the Lord and how He can carry us through.

"I am making very slow progress now and one of my problems has been waiting on the Lord for patience to get better. One thing seems to keep other things back, and it was hard to see the way forward for a while there, but just in the last few days I feel I see a light in the end of the tunnel, and words of encouragement from the doctors and physios etc at how well I am doing is really motivating me. I am determined to get as fit as possible and sometimes tire myself too much and have to be reminded a little progress every day is better than huge determination and disappointment.

"Thank you all so much for your continued prayers, cards, gifts etc. It has been a tremendous testimony to the nurses the fact that I have so many people interested and praying for me and I have had so many comments from them even when in ICU and I couldn't talk - that was a trial for me!! When they first put a voice box on my trachy it was like pure bliss to be able to communicate again.

"I could go on forever, I have so much I could tell you but all in good time. The Lord has been good and I hope I can give you more positive feedback in the near future. Love in our Lord, Audrey."

With more strength for writing, she had now evicted Adrian from the computer and began to communicate further.

"Just to let you know how my visit to Newcastle went on Tuesday. Well, the doctors all seemed to be happy with my progress and I got home the same day again - hurrah!! My exercising must have helped as my lung capacity has increased in the 10 days since I was last tested and is now at FEV1 1.02 which is about 40% of predicted for the new lung. I asked if this was a normal improvement and the doctor just said I was obviously doing all the right things as he was pleased with that considering my rocky start. He did say it will take about a year for the lung to reach its full capacity, so I just need to be patient. It is great though to be walking about, on the treadmill for 10 mins, bike for 15 mins, weights etc each day with no oxygen on and still not too out of breath!

"My oxygen sats are also looking great. I was sitting at 100% O2 saturation at rest the other day - even Adrian is only 95% so I can tease him about that.

"The surgical emphysema has now almost gone away, I think, as there is not much in the way of crackling now under my skin, but I still have a big round face - it's the result of the steroids, but these are coming down each week also so I hope my face decreases in size too. I am starting to feel more 'normal' each day. I was in a few shops today for a little retail therapy and was not conscious of anyone staring at me - they probably just assume I've been eating too many biscuits!!

"My fitness levels are getting better each day and my body doesn't feel just the deadweight it was when I came out of hospital - the muscles are beginning to support much better. I like to push out the boundaries each day to see what happens and I'm pleased to say I am now back to cooking simple meals which don't take too much preparation, sitting on my perching stool when necessary but enjoying the independence that this brings. I am looking forward to the day when I can drive again and really feel my independence. I believe they do say about 3 months - so that's only 3 weeks away!! Just to give you a laugh, I wanted some wrapping paper out of my hallway cupboard today and it was on the floor at the back of the cupboard. I wondered if I could reach it - so I thought 'let's give it a go!' As I had to bend my legs quite far to get down, my muscles gave way and down I went on my bottom to which my mother-in-law came running. I then had the problem of trying to get up off the floor again! Ah well, all in good time!

"I am also looking forward to getting out to the meetings again. I can't at the moment as I have to avoid infections at all costs until I get my strength back a bit and as you probably know everyone is coming down with colds just now. Again they say 12 weeks, but I will have to ask around as to how many are under the weather and move my seat when appropriate - seems very rude but a nasty bug could set me back a long way.

"I apologise if my blogs have been a bit more gushy than usual. I am finding that this is another thing which this experience has taught me. Why are we so reserved in our feelings towards people? I always felt shy about praising people or telling them how much I loved them before, but I find now that I am able to see the good in people much more and tell them! I don't think it's such a bad thing really! I always thought it was sad that we often waited until a person's funeral service to give them a glowing report - wouldn't it have been nicer to tell them to their face while they were still here! Let's shine a bit of love around - it may just make someone's day!"

As Audrey steadily improved, her check-ups in Newcastle held less dread. It became a great shock, however, when she discovered she was having another lung rejection episode. She began to write,

"As you know I had another clinic visit at Freeman's on Monday/Tuesday this week. I went down feeling great and wanting to show the doctors how much I had improved with my exercise regime etc, but unfortunately the outcome was not as good this time. The first alert sign was when I went for lung function tests and they were slightly down on 10 days previous! I was really surprised and one of the doctors said to me 'Maybe you have reached your maximum and will stay at that' - that did not encourage me at all! However, when they did the bronchoscopy on Monday, they discovered I was having another rejection. I, therefore, have had to stay in hospital until yesterday as they had to blast me with IV steroids again for 3 days and put me in isolation again with reverse barrier nursing. I must say I was quite deflated as I had being doing so well and I felt like I was on a snakes and ladders board - the problem is the further up the board you go the longer the snakes seem to be and you fall harder. On the plus side though I am not back at square one - my fitness levels are still much better than last time and I'm home again! As the Prof said, he needs to nip these problems in the bud so that I can enjoy 20 years on my new lung - and that's just a start he said - that will suit me fine!

"As I was considering the nuisance of losing home comforts and being kept away from company for another few weeks, I thought about the Lord. I was reading in Psalm 2 of how God has promised the Lord an inheritance in His saints. I thought of how He chose to leave His home with all the splendours of

Heaven, for 33 years, to suffer the despising and rejecting of men, all so that He could win His bride back to himself. I was humbled by this sacrifice and it made my suffering pale into insignificance - what a God that He would do this for us - I don't feel worthy of that sacrifice!

"The first night I was on steroids I only slept for 3 hours and then my mind was running again, so I decided to read in Ephesians - what a mine of jewels I received from God to help me - I will share that with you tomorrow. Just wanting to update you on the basic progress just now and catch up-to-date with home life. Thanks for your continued prayers."

After this second rejection episode, her medication was changed. The large bullet type pills, with the peculiar and unpleasant smell were replaced by another wonder drug, this time encapsulated in tiny pills. The change of drugs marked the end of the initial two rejections Audrey had suffered.

Towards the end of November 2008, Audrey had a further hospital visit to Newcastle for a consultation with Professor Corris who had followed her problems with great interest and had led her medical team. He outlined the gravity of what she had been through: "Audrey, to explain, it is like you have fallen off a railway bridge and landed on the road below, only to have been hit by a truck when you lay on the road. This is an apt description of the start you had with the new lung. It did not want to work at first and you are going to be one of the ones that takes a long time to recover because of this – perhaps a year. But go out there with a smile on your face at how well you are doing."

With the Professor's words ringing in her ears, she left the hospital with a beaming smile and a skip in her step. She was relieved that it was six weeks until the next time she would be due in Newcastle. She could now enjoy Christmas and New Year at home in Methven and not in hospital.

Now that the rejection episode had passed, she was now ready to start meeting people again. Just minutes before the service at Perth Gospel Hall commenced, she slipped in at the back. She was so pleased to hear God's Word again and to meet up with the Lord's people. For 3 months she had not been able to be with them and had missed them sorely. Her next aim was to be able to enjoy the Lord's Supper on the following Sunday morning. She loved to remember her Lord; it was His command, "This do in remembrance of me."

Sunday arrived and she took her place with the friends at the Gospel Hall. In the months of her absence a few things had changed. Two of the members had died, one very suddenly. She wondered at the ways of God, that they had died but she had lived. She was determined to live now, counting every day as a gift from God.

On the Saturday afternoon, the family decided that it would be a great tonic after the stresses of the previous months if they had some games of badminton and table tennis at the local Sports Centre. Audrey sat patiently watching from her wheelchair for a while but couldn't resist getting involved. Before long she was having a few games of table tennis. Adrian even challenged her to a game only to discover she had lost little of her winning spirit.

Christmas 2008 arrived. Audrey and Adrian enjoyed this very special day together. It was the day they had thought they could never spend together, but God had mercifully overruled. Their day started with prayer and a Bible reading about the Wise Men. Adrian commented, "Can you imagine the joy that these men had when they saw the star which led them to the Saviour. It is lovely to read that they fell down and worshipped Him. The babe in the manger is the Son of God and the Saviour of the World."

The Christmas day lunch was a wonderful celebration of the day and Audrey's recovering health. Moira hosted the family with 20 people sitting down to enjoy the feast. Family games followed, with musical entertainment from talented nephews.

Next day the family gathered at the Fergusons and Audrey and Adrian, with many helpers, catered for them. Audrey was delighted that she could again host such a happy time, so soon after her life saving lung transplant. Adrian found a quiet moment and penned a poem to share about their experiences. He stood up and shared 17 verses of his "Ode to Audrey". His final verse summarised the year:

> *Now as we reflect on the year that's near gone,*
> *It's been a hard journey and it seems very long.*
> *But lifting our eyes and our hearts in this squall,*
> *We still praise our dear Saviour, the Maker of all.*

A tradition for many Christians at the turn of the year is to attend Bible teaching conferences, to commence a new year with their souls nourished by the changeless Word of God. Audrey was determined to get to as many conferences at possible, crammed into three very busy days. At one conference there was such a queue of people waiting to see her that it was nearly late at re-commencing. So many had prayed for her that she personally wanted to thank as many as possible. A New Year had commenced. Audrey was excited about the days that would lie ahead.

CHAPTER 15

Getting Going Again

Adrian returned to his job in mid October 2008. He had left in a hurry, his colleagues very much "holding the baby". They had managed to continue the success of the department and he began to wonder, "Am I really needed here?" He was soon to learn that there was still plenty to do in the office. A very large and challenging project arrived on his desk. He was determined to make a success of it. Here was an opportunity to save the company tens of millions of pounds - if the project could be completed successfully.

Audrey was taking the first few steps towards feeling normal again. She rejoiced at how God had kept His promise from Jeremiah 29:11 and given her "hope and a future". She was determined to find out what that plan for her life would be. Her mind turned to help stabilise the core of the Sunday School. Throughout the UK many Sunday Schools have closed due to a dwindling core, with even the core dropping off and the Sunday School closing. They began to seek ideas from other Sunday School leaders and eventually settled on an incentive plan - a free day trip. The plan was that over the next five weeks, a child had to come at least four times - no excuses, except hospitalisation were permitted! The plan was simple to explain and simple to coordinate. It proved to be an immediate success with the children. The regular children became even better attenders, while some on the periphery became regular. One lad who had to visit his father every second week, made special plans to come back early to ensure he never missed Sunday School.

Meantime the leaders were puzzling over the destination for the trip. They decided on Deep Sea World in North Queensferry. Audrey had started thinking about every aspect - safety, lunch, transport, and her specialism - getting a reduced entry fee! Adrian's only job was to ensure the bus was booked to take the children the 30 miles there. After phoning around, the company with the cheapest price was decided on. This proved to be an interesting decision!

The day of the trip finally arrived, and the children and leaders set off in a brand new bus along the motorway towards Deep Sea World. Less than 15 miles out of Perth, the bus started to alarm – stop immediately! The driver pulled over - it appeared to be leaking oil. Now the leaders had a bus full of children parked on a busy motorway, with the Fergusons ahead in a car with the food. The leaders entertained the children with singing and stories, but as they waited for a replacement bus, a few started to cry needing a comfort stop. Wonderfully a replacement bus came just at the right time, and all the children were escorted to the nearest roadside service station. When the bus finally arrived at the Centre, smoke and steam were billowing from the engine. Once the children were safely inside and enjoying their lunch and tour, Adrian had an opportunity to speak to the driver. "What's the chance of us getting home without a further breakdown?" He replied rather dishearteningly, "Oh, there's a 90% probability!" "I'm not looking for 90%, I need 100% probability!" Adrian replied. The driver shrugged his shoulders.

The time came to head home. The bus chugged away and this time Audrey followed the bus in her car. A few miles into the journey and the bus was starting to lose water from its radiator, then a few more miles, the water was steam, then a few more miles and the steam was starting to dry up! One more hill and we will be almost home, but then instead of steam, smoke poured out of the back of the bus and the children were starting to cough due to the smoke inside the bus. The driver had no option but to pull over as the engine had stopped in this second bus. Now they were stuck on a motorway again, with the light fading and a bus full of children to entertain. Audrey as usual was quick thinking, "I'll take the leaders back to Perth, and they can return with their cars to shuttle the children home." So Adrian and a couple of leaders were to try and entertain these increasingly restless children while the rest of them dashed back for their cars.

The third bus of the day arrived – and remarkably it didn't break down as it returned the last few children home safely. Off they skipped, happy with their adventure in three buses and at the Deep Sea World. The next day at Sunday School the children were all excited about their trip while the leaders managed to make light of the unusual circumstances!

When Monday came, Adrian called the bus company to raise his concerns. They were considerate and the Gospel Hall received a full refund. But they had lost two buses, had to use three drivers, pay for two rescue lorries to retrieve buses off the motorway, and then refund the customer. Not much profit for them! It was yet another exciting post-transplant experience, and a lesson that cheapest is not always best!

After the trials of 2008, Audrey planned a spring holiday for 2009; it would be just the tonic they required! She had heard that Shropshire was very picturesque, and planned action filled days exploring. Once on holiday, the tree pollen was building up and Adrian needed hay fever medication. He had bought the "non drowsy" variety but within minutes of taking it, he became completely exhausted. He would sleep for nearly twelve hours, eat breakfast, and then fall asleep again. He would rise for lunch, then feel drowsy again as they planned to go out for a drive. One day in Shrewsbury Adrian was pushing Audrey in the wheelchair. She hadn't used it for weeks, she had been walking everywhere and didn't need it, but Shrewsbury is built on a hill and she decided to use the wheelchair. Adrian must have gone soft as he could barely cope with pushing it around. He found a park bench to get another sleep. Audrey decided enough was enough; "Get in!" she said - she would push him! It was quite a sight: Adrian dozing in the chair with Audrey just about to push him around the town. Role reversal was visible at its finest.

Easter weekend 2009 became a real highlight, when it had been decided to hold a special mini-camp. They had missed only one mini-camp due to the transplant and were excited to get involved again. Audrey did the administration of the application forms and the camp fees, delighted to be able to use her admin skills again. Adrian organised Easter themed ideas, with the leaders sharing in the fun activities. The guest speaker was Ivan McLean from Ahoghill in Northern Ireland. He had been deeply involved in youth outreach and was pleased to be able to use his holidays to come and speak to the campers. Many would never have heard preaching like this before, nothing light hearted, but powerful and Christ exalting. He had a burden from God that the campers would be presented with the message of life. At the camp, Audrey had offered to give a talk about her transplant to anyone that wanted to hear about it. This was an optional extra, but 70 people turned up to hear her describe emotionally what she had gone through, and the hand of God upon her. She wasn't preaching, but her words came with real love for the young people and for her God. She had prayed that some would be touched by what she had gone through in the last months and that God would save some. God did bless the camp and one girl confessed that she had trusted in Christ. The Fergusons viewed it as evidence of God's continuing hand upon them.

Audrey was making steady progress but had no plans of returning to her previous career in banking. She was one of the youngest pensioners ever and was enjoying her more leisurely life. The bank, though, had forgotten to remove her from some of their lists. One evening her phone rang. "Hello, it's the Royal Bank, can you please go to the Perth branch and reload the cash machine." She laughed, "I retired years ago, I think you will need to check your list!" She was now more in the habit of emptying cash machines, rather than filling them!

Throughout Scotland there was a deep and continued interest in Audrey's illness and miraculous recovery. Every meeting they attended, many people said, "We pray for you every day." These were genuine comments from both friends and strangers who had made it their habit to pray earnestly for them. One Thursday evening, a friend telephoned to invite Adrian to give a public talk on the subject of Audrey's transplant. This would be the first opportunity to do this, and Adrian agreed to go. The only problem was that it was another very busy week at home, and time to prepare the talk was severely limited. The night before was the first opportunity to start preparing. Quickly he pulled his thoughts together into a very rough presentation. When Friday came the venue quickly filled up with the audience looking forward to hearing the story of "a life saving lung transplant". Adrian paused, it was strange to stand before such a crowd with no script and just a few slides to aid one's thoughts. He stood up trusting in the Lord and his knees knocking. The Lord's help was real, and it was only when the video was published on the internet that Adrian realised he had spoken for an hour and eight minutes! Many were touched by the talk, and a few more invitations came to give it again as far north as Aberdeen and as far south as Newcastle.

The difficulties of Audrey's illness had made a real impact on some of her own family. Her niece Katie and her nephew David had been totally shocked when her condition was so critical. The night when everything seemed grim, Katie had taken her sister Emma's whiteboard and penned the words, "Pray for Audrey" and placed it near her window so that all could see. She wanted the whole world to pray for Audrey. Katie was soon to realise that God did answer prayer. With the power of God shown to David and Katie, they began to consider obeying their Lord further. They agreed they would show others their faith in Christ by being baptised. On the Sunday of the baptism the hall filled with friends, family and their congregation. One of the church elders asked both of them why they were being baptised and both related their testimony to Christ as Saviour and how Audrey's transplant had shaken their lives to the core. Audrey's eyes welled up with tears, she would go through it all again for the opportunities she had received to witness for her Lord.

Sharon Grant, a family friend was celebrating her 40th birthday in 2009. Her husband asked her, "Sharon, what do you want for your 40th?" She replied, "I would like to walk the West Highland Way and raise funds for LAM Action, Audrey's favoured charity." Sharon and Stephen decided they could actually get a team of walkers together and raise more funds for LAM Action. Within a few weeks they had assembled a large team who gallantly trekked over 100 miles. When the blisters came and the fatigue set in, one of the comics replied, "I won't give in, I'm doing it for Audrey!" They joked, "Our blisters are for Audrey!" When she called them to ask what supplies she could bring them at the half-way mark, they all replied, "Blister plasters!"

The "over the hill walkers" completed the course and Audrey watched as the funds continued to rise. Eventually almost £10,000 was raised. The LAM Action team looked with delight at the cheque, it was the biggest donation they had ever received.

During Audrey's years of illness, she had been responsible for arranging the regular school outreach in Perthshire. This entailed writing, phoning and booking schools to have a guest Christian speaker. As her illness had progressed, her calls had to be made accompanied by the background noise of her oxygen on the phone line. Now free from that, she approached this task with renewed gusto. The school staff were deeply interested in her story and she wondered if perhaps she could start meeting some of these teachers. Checking the school diary she found an opportune time to go into a school with Adrian who would conduct the assembly, where the children would enjoy the singing and a Bible story. As he started to tidy up, the Head Teacher appeared and Audrey stepped forward and began to chat. For the next 30 minutes she shared her experiences and stories. Her approach was exactly what was needed to be able to get close to the Head Teacher. A few months later, a Christian Trust donated a Children's Bible to every pupil in the school. They did not have a local representative but wanted a Christian to go into the school to present the Bibles. The school said, "We will ask Audrey to present them!" She was glad to agree, then the Head Teacher said, "Oh, and you can tell them what the Bible is all about, and give them a story." Audrey gulped, she wasn't sure if she should conduct a school assembly, but with the insistence of the teachers she was committed!

In the days before the occasion Audrey wondered what she should tell them. Her mind was still not as clear thinking, or her memory as sharp as she would have liked it to be. Adrian suggested, "Tell them what the Bible is about and I'll tell them a story from it. Tell how it's the best seller; it's a mirror, a sword, a light and a lamp. Tell how it teaches us wisdom and truth, but especially tell them it points us to the Lord Jesus." On some fluorescent card they began to write information about the Bible. "Stick these on a large board and use them to aid your memory", encouraged Adrian.

The school assembly started and Audrey was introduced to the children. She was nervous but they sat and listened intently as she explained about the wonderful Bible and her precious Saviour. Only a few months previously she was fighting for her very existence, now she was pressing forward in service for God. At the end, she handed out the Bibles and everyone went home with this priceless treasure in their hands. She prayed it would soon be found in their hearts.

During the few months before Audrey's transplant, a new Gospel Hall in Perth was being purchased. The property was a rundown hotel function suite, which was in need of total renovation. It was smoke-stained, dirty and smelled of beer, having been used for weddings, auctions, even boxing. Audrey followed the progress of the work all through her recuperation and as soon as she was able, she paid a surprise visit to see it. Donning her hard hat, she walked into the building site, to meet the builders. She was delighted to see the progress. Having prayed for an appropriate place for the Christians to meet, the answer was being revealed. When May 2009 arrived, the hall was ready to be opened and Audrey was delighted to be at the very first service held in it. The new hall gave a fresh impetus for the Christians to reach their neighbours for the Lord. Audrey helped by inviting the neighbours into the hall, knocking on doors and using her own experience to witness for her Lord. She was shocked at how few people wanted to hear about the Lord Jesus.

The elders in the Gospel Hall had another idea to reach their neighbourhood - organising a Bible exhibition. They asked Audrey to organise the schools and all the administration of the exhibition. She was pleased to be able to use her time at home to best effect, planning it like a military expedition, with detailed records, e-mails, letters and a phone call diary. There were buses to organise, schools to contact, volunteer leaders to train and snacks to be made. She enjoyed using her skills in God's service. When the exhibition arrived, the committee were amazed at all the planning that she had completed. They were so impressed they even asked her to join their committee!

Week by week, new people were coming into the Gospel Hall and Audrey was praying that many would trust the Lord. He was in fact saving souls as the message was preached to young and old, and she was pleased how her prayers were being answered.

Perhaps the biggest evidence of her returning health was not before a large crowd, it was before a handful of children. With a few children before her she took a Sunday School class for the first time in years, a substitute teacher for one Sunday. Despite her own difficulties she still loved to tell the children about the

Lord Jesus. As she reached this high point, she wondered what would be round the corner. She would be shocked as the next series of events in her roller coaster experience began to unfold.

CHAPTER 16

The Unknown Future

As 2009 commenced, there were many days when Audrey felt she had been fighting the heavyweight boxing champion of the world. Her body felt heavy, her lung area was still sore, her legs were weak and her concentration had evaporated. She was certainly battered and bruised. Thankfully as the year swiftly progressed every day became a step forward. The progress Audrey was making was soon visible for everyone to see. "You look so healthy," was the regular comment. Even strangers could barely believe that she had had a lung transplant. Being disabled had given Audrey some helpful perks, one of which was a disabled parking permit, giving her exclusive parking spaces, all at no cost. With improving health, she had no desire to continue being disabled. "I cannot justify this anymore," - and she cut up her permit and threw it in the rubbish bin. Another era was over for her - chronic disability was hopefully a thing of the past.

With all the excitement of the past few years, quiet moments of reflection were always at a premium. She had learned that quietness and contemplation was something which required effort. In one quiet moment, she recalled the little song she often sang as a carefree teenager,

> *"Leave the unknown future in the Master's hands;*
> *Whether sad or joyful Jesus understands."*

She was learning that every day the unknown future must be left there.

As early summer was approaching, enthusiastically she began planning to attend the annual LAM Action conference. "The guest speaker is Professor Corris," she announced. "He was amazing at caring for me; I'd love to hear what he has to say at the conference." This would be the first time she could meet her LAM friends, post-transplant and celebrate with them. Then she heard the news that there would be four ladies attending the conference who had recently had transplants. In a tiny community, this was surely the largest gathering of post-transplant LAM patients ever! She was excited to meet others who also had experienced the gift of life. To her surprise a press photographer came to record this momentous day. Audrey smiled, so pleased that her life had been spared.

During free time at the conference she spotted something that would further help her recovery - an electric bike. "Adrian, I think I'll order one of these - then I can race you round the block," she said. After searching for the best price, within a few days the new bike arrived. True to her word she was soon racing Adrian around the country lanes. With this device, whenever she needed an extra boost the battery took over and she could whizz effortlessly along the road, With Adrian left trailing in her dust. She no longer felt she had a disability. He replied stoically, "I'll need to buy a faster bike!"

In June, just as life was returning to normal, she started to experience considerable pain, concentrated in her lower back, making sleep difficult with the ache it left. At one of her routine appointments in Perth, she mentioned this to her consultant. He was unwilling to dismiss it as just another routine symptom without first giving her a fuller examination. He arranged for an ultrasound scan of liver and kidneys, and a further CT scan of her spine. These scans gave great concern to the clinician. He explained to Audrey that there was a growth on her kidney and liver as well as some problems at the base of her spine. It was feared that these might be cancerous tumours. These can be one of the severe side effects of the immuno suppressants. It was now vital to get it checked.

Further consultations were arranged with the specialists in Newcastle, and Audrey waited for the appointment card to arrive. The appointments were right in the middle of two of the highlights of her year - the Perth Gospel Hall Bible Study week and the Senior Camp week. She could hardly believe the timing. "I'll call and ask if they can move the appointment by a week." When she called, the answer was, "This is too important to move, if these are cancerous every minute matters. I think you should come as planned." Now she was concerned. "Too important to move - that sounds more serious than I imagined." She stood facing yet another life threatening prognosis. "They had promised it would be like a roller coaster ride - they certainly were true to their word," she said as she headed off to Newcastle for further examinations. The friends at the Gospel Hall prayed earnestly that it would not be more bad news. She had learned the importance of surrounding herself with prayer partners and had felt the lasting benefit of it.

The whirr of the MRI scanner started and she was drawn through this powerful machine. She laughed at the memory of a previous experience in a scanner like this. Lying flat on the bed as she passed into the machine her feet spontaneously started to lift up into the air. She wondered, "What's happening? I've lost control of my limbs!" The technician quickly replied, "Don't worry - you must have metal plates in your shoes!" Shoes were removed and the scan started in earnest. It was amazing how radio signals along with such huge magnets could be used to create an image of her organs. She was even more amazed that such a device had been invented only during her lifetime. Medical science had made marvellous strides forward, many of which she had benefited from.

The consultant pathologists and radiologists examined the images. The pain in her spine was from a fractured vertebra, possibly as a result of either her car crash or the period when she had to be manually turned in intensive care. Only time would heal this. She had two growths on her kidneys also and further growths on her liver. The big question was, "But are they cancerous?" The consultants' response - "Thankfully, no, these are consistent with angiolipoma growths present in LAM".

What a relief, her symptoms were from her original disease not any new sinister development. Delighted, she was free to return home and continue the Bible Study week.

Now with a spring in her step, she threw herself back into all the activities planned for the summer. "It will be camp next week; it should be an exciting time." The camp theme was based on the financial crisis sweeping the world economy - a "Credit Crunch Christian Camp". It had seemed like a strange choice, but it caught the imagination of the campers and became another successful week. The only disadvantage for Audrey was that she had to sit for 30 minutes each morning and night, hooked up to a nebuliser. This was to help treat her for the trace of pseudomonas that had been found in her lungs.

After a few weeks of the nebuliser, her tongue's appearance began to change dramatically. "Adrian, look at this, there is something wrong!" It had changed from a healthy pink to a ghostly white, the edge marked by strange growths which refused to clear up with ointment or mouth-wash. "What's happening now?" she sighed. Her local consultant patiently explained that it would need further investigation in case it was serious. An emergency appointment was arranged at the Dundee dental hospital.

Once there, she struggled to find a car parking space - the only space available was limited to one hour. The consultant closely examined her tongue. He wondered if the problem could be "Graft Versus Host disease", which is the opposite of lung rejection when the body rejects the lung; now the lung could be rejecting the body. In this disease as the lung rejects the body, it begins to damage the body, killing cells in the organs and can often manifest itself in the tongue first. Audrey had survived LAM, a complex transplant, a cancer scare - and now she was facing another life threatening challenge. She refused to be downhearted, she even laughed, "I think I've had my fair share of serious conditions for one person. Adrian, you pay the taxes and I spend them!"

As the consultation proceeded, Audrey started to panic. "I'll have to get another parking ticket on my car." The consultant, a renowned expert, paused, "If you don't mind, I'll go and put the ticket on your car. It will save you a walk." She gasped, "That would be a wonderful help". When he returned he said, "I hope you don't mind, I noticed your music CDs and I want to tell you, whatever the outcome of today, you're in good hands!" Her heart was lifted. The consultant was a believer who had recognised her Christian music. The Lord had sent encouragement in the middle of another crisis. The consultant had one further procedure to complete. He apologised, "I'm sorry but I'll have to cut a bit off your tongue to do a biopsy." So she was now literally tongue tied, with stitches hanging out of her tongue. Adrian would laugh "Have you nothing to say tonight?" - she could only respond with a lisping groan!

An anxious few days passed waiting for the results. "What will they find?" she wondered. At last - "Audrey you have a condition called Hairy Leukoplakia. It is normally associated with AIDS patients, but in your case, it is linked to your low immune system, your steroids and the use of nebulised antibiotics." She was puzzled, "So what have I to do?" "Let's try you off the nebuliser and see if there is any improvement." His diagnosis was perfect, stopping the nebuliser had an almost instant effect on her tongue, it soon began to look more normal again. The scares of the summer had passed without any lasting damage.

Audrey started to dream about a celebratory holiday. "Let's have a Baltic Cruise!" She set about planning the agenda: "We can even meet some Christian friends in Norway." In Norway, a further contact in Finland was arranged: she rejoiced, "Christian company, on holiday this is great." After Finland, her friends from Norway sent a surprise message, "We've arranged for another Christian to meet you in Estonia!" She was excited that so many dedicated Christians were willing to guide her round their countries.

After their adventures on the high seas, Audrey and Adrian returned to normal life again. Normal life, although busy, was rewarding and full of joy for them. One quiet evening Audrey announced, "I've decided I'm ready to write a letter to thank the family of the lung donor." She knew so little about her donor - anonymity was guaranteed by the hospital. The protocol was that a letter could be sent to the hospital, who would then pass it on to the donor family. If the donor family wished to respond they could do so but only via the hospital. She carefully prepared what she would write, then paused and reflected that every happy anniversary for her was a sad one for the donor's family. She realised that someone she never knew had died, and that death had allowed her to live. She bowed her head to thank God for the life she now had. Nor could she forget the comparison with her Saviour, who had died that she might live eternally.

Feeling stronger every day, she was able to get involved in the outreach programme the believers at Perth Gospel Hall had planned for the autumn. They had decided to try and run a "Christianity Explored" class, where people could explore the Christian faith in an informal environment. They started to work out who they could invite. "Let's try and visit some of the Sunday School parents, perhaps they will come." As they visited, they were pleased that some of their contacts were willing to attend the special class. Audrey wondered if they would all come. She was so pleased that all who had promised, actually turned up. Over 20 non members of the Gospel Hall came to hear about the Bible in this friendly and informal manner. Adrian had visited a mother of a Sunday School child, "Would you like to come?" "Yes, I'll come if you can pick me up." She came with her daughter and her nephew, producing a further challenge - now there were children to look after while sharing the scriptures with their parents. One of the young ladies volunteered and arranged crafts and games for the young ones. Another lady was visited who had a drug addiction problem. Adrian just told her very straight, "This is exactly what you need!" To his amazement she came the first night and soon she began to follow the Lord. They were pleased that their circle of contacts was growing and the gospel of the Lord Jesus Christ was still spreading in Scotland.

These autumn months also saw another new venture for the Gospel Hall - a mother and toddlers group. The "Little Treasures" began with just a small group of children and mothers, but quickly grew until the hall was full. Audrey wondered, "How can we bring the Bible into this group more effectively?" One of her friends supplied the words of some children's choruses and she arranged for them to be printed for them. They sat around and began to sing God's praise in the ears of little children and their parents. With a regular singing spot organised, they thought they would try a story with these young children. Audrey was happy to volunteer and even tried her hand at telling the story with her puppet Hamish.

Audrey's enthusiasm for reaching the young was increasing as her health improved. Phoning to book school assemblies, two of the largest ones could not be fitted into the schedule. Anxious not to miss an opportunity, she said, "Oh Adrian can come instead of the visiting speaker!" The first one was held in a packed hall with nearly 470 pupils and teachers crammed in. He told the story from Acts 12 about Peter in prison, then related the story of Audrey's transplant and how God had answered their prayers. The children and teachers were amazed to see this living witness to answered prayer. Only a week after this assembly, they were shocked to hear that the Local Authority had condemned that assembly hall: "A maximum of 60 people should be in the hall at one time". Adrian chuckled, "Oh well, they were only 400 above the limit when I spoke!" Two weeks later, they were back in another Perth school, privileged to speak again about their Saviour and the power of prayer. A thousand children in two weeks had heard about the Lord Jesus!

Throughout the country, people were keen to hear Adrian tell the story of Audrey's lung transplant. One of the most memorable occasions was in great contrast to the 1000 children in Perth. He was invited to Avoch on the Black Isle to give a talk in their community centre. They spent Sunday with the Christians the Gospel Hall there, with a total of six people partaking in the Lord's Supper. They wondered if only four locals attended then, how many would come at night? To their surprise, the hall was filled with over 80 people coming to listen. The local Christians had worked hard to invite their neighbours and friends. Audrey and Adrian remarked, "It was like revival had broken out - nearly 15 times increase over the morning service!"

The spring of 2010 brought an opportunity for a welcome holiday in Spain. Audrey planned a cheap week for some spring sunshine in Fuengirola, a perfect rest for them both. As they walked along the promenade in the warm evening air, Audrey said, "We'll be home tomorrow, back to the rain of Scotland!" It suddenly seemed less attractive than the balmy air of Spain! But back at their hotel, news came through that all flights to the UK were cancelled due to some volcanic ash cloud. They hadn't ever heard about a volcanic cloud causing flight problems! "It'll be fine tomorrow," they assured each other. The cloud, though, refused to move and Europe's airports were closed down. For the first time since the Wright brothers, only birds were permitted to fly!

Day after day, they waited for news, but they were getting an extended holiday - free! On Sunday, they attended the local English speaking Evangelical Church. The tiny congregation was greatly increased with stranded holiday makers seeking assurance and comfort from the Bible. The main speaker greeted Adrian at the door and asked, "Would you please read the scripture passage today and give a brief word of testimony?" He shared a little of the story of his life with Christ and some of their recent experiences. The few words proved to be a help to so many upset and stranded passengers. Looking around the audience, he was sure that some were in the same hotel as they were. Back at the hotel, they met up with their new friends - an

Independent Methodist Pastor, a Baptist, a Salvation Army lady, and two Scottish Free Presbyterians. This unusual experience was a warm and genuinely happy one for them, miles from home but at home with God's people.

The ash cloud stayed stubbornly in the sky, and after nearly an extra week the tour operator agreed to bus everyone back from Spain to Glasgow Airport. That would be a gruelling journey, to travel from the farthest south of Europe north into Scotland, but there were no other options. The first stage from Fuengirola to Pineda de Mar took nearly 17 hours. They arrived at the hotel at 4am, with only one receptionist and 200 guests to process. The hotel had been opened especially for the stranded tourists. It was so cold that the bed felt damp, and when Adrian got into bed, he soon realised that he had extra company - the bed bugs began to bite. He lay there and thought, "If the missionaries can manage, so should I!" His determination was weak though. Within minutes he got fully dressed again and tucked his socks into his trousers to prevent the vermin accessing his legs.

In the morning, he went to find out when they were to depart for the next long journey through France to Calais. At reception, he learned that the plan had changed again! It was to be a further journey across Spain to Bilbao and then a cruise home. The thought of a luxury cruise appeals to most, but he was frustrated by now and wondered if they should make their own way home. He phoned his brother for advice. The sage advice was, "Sit tight, it is brand new cruise ship and you are the first passengers!" The smile returned and the next day they boarded the *Celebrity Eclipse* on its maiden voyage from Bilbao to Southampton. At the room allocation, Adrian joked, "Can we have the honeymoon suite?" The lady smiled in reply; she had probably heard the same request 1000 times! They did receive a beautiful luxury balcony cabin, but they kept quiet about it when they heard of real honeymooners getting single beds in an inside cabin! There was more - as a goodwill gesture the cruise company gave them $55 on-board credit. Audrey was able to purchase presents for the family and even a bottle of perfume for herself. Adrian got the pleasure of watching her spend someone else's money!

* * * * * * *

The experiences Audrey had passed through were strangely reflected in a short poem Adrian had written for the Sunday School children to recite, long before these dark days. He could never have known how they would both learn to apply these words in their trials.

The Light of the World – by Adrian Ferguson

In days of darkness Jesus stood,
Amidst the toil and strife,
He gently said, "Come follow me,
I am the light of life."

In days of sorrow Jesus said,
"When all around is bleak,
I am the light that millions know,
And which you're wise to seek."

In days of sickness Jesus touched
The lonely and distressed,
His gentle words were heard to say,
"In Me is sweetest rest."

In days of laughter and delight,
The Saviour's light shines on,
In joyful days my heart proclaims,
"His light will be my song."

Each day the Saviour's light is seen,
From God's own Word declared,
The lamp, the light, the brightest joy,
No other light compares!

When next you're plunged into the dark,
And wondering what to do,
Just call upon His blessed name,
He'll be the light for you.

One thing that has deeply impressed Audrey through all her experiences has been the number of people who earnestly state, "I pray for you every day." She is overwhelmed that there are hundreds, some whom she barely knows, who are daily seeking God's blessing on her. Every day is a testament to what God has done. One of her LAM friends beautifully summarised it: "You are a living evidence of the power of prayer, medical expertise and positive thinking." Her survival had been a trial of immense proportions, but she rejoices that the "Great Physician" had guided even the surgeon's hands.

Her latest consultation at Freeman's hospital in Newcastle was perhaps the highlight of all such visits, and a fitting conclusion to this part of her story. After extensive tests, the consultant collated the results and read them carefully to her. To her delight, she had attained her best statistics since her transplant. Audrey quietly paused and praised God for His unfailing love.

She could joyfully say she was, "Kept Safely Kept".